TIME ON A TINY ISLAND

MY PEACE CORPS ODYSSEY

For G-d and the journey.
For my loved ones out there in the Pacific,
for reminding me we are connected across the ocean.

Copyright © 2025 by Amy Muscoplat

All rights reserved. No part of this book may be reproduced or used in any manner without written permission of the copyright owner except for the use of quotations in a book review. For more information, contact: amy@joyfestivalindustries.com

Published by Joyfestival Industries.

First edition January 2025

Book design by the Virtual Paintbrush.

ISBN 979-8-9924675-0-5 (hardcover)
ISBN 979-8-9924675-1-2 (paperback)
ISBN 979-8-9924675-2-9 (ebook)

joyfestivalindustries.com

TIME ON A TINY ISLAND

MY PEACE CORPS ODYSSEY

AMY MUSCOPLAT

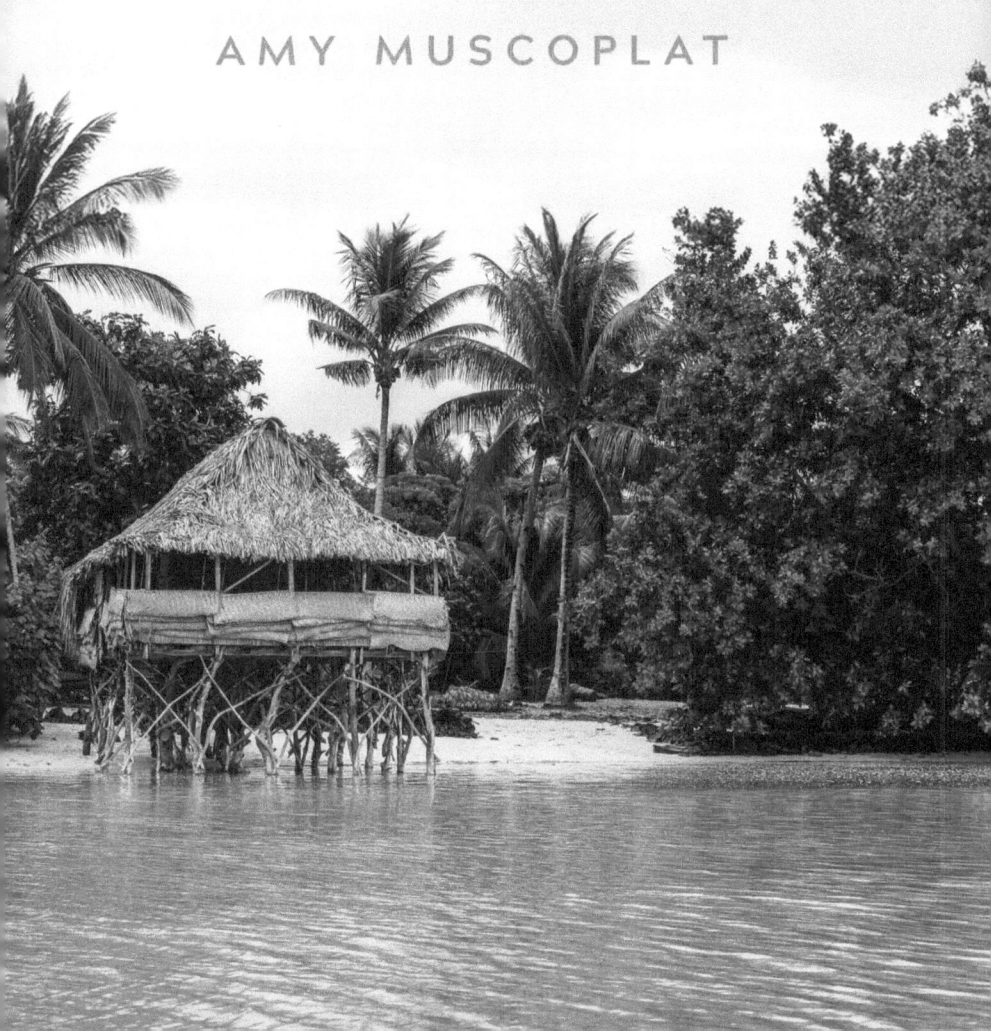

AUTHOR'S NOTE

The names of those people involved in my story and my experiences in Kiribati and beyond have been changed to respect their privacy. Thank you all for enriching my life.

PROLOGUE

Straight out of graduate school in December 1995, at age twenty-five, I have scored what my father calls a "good job." I am not happy in this role. I am a news research librarian for a daily newspaper in South Florida, where I help reporters find the background material they need on people, places, events, and other news items. I have good benefits, and the salary is not bad. The projects I work on are usually interesting, but my main job is finding the latest information from courts or public records on people involved in the latest murder, rape, child abuse case, or the like. It is incredibly depressing, and not creative or meaningful to me.

Because I'm working at a daily paper, everyone is always on tight deadlines; they need things *right* now—or fifteen minutes ago. It's chaotic and not very pleasant. I'm not sleeping well, and then the guy I'm dating, who writes for the paper, goes a little crazy when I break up with him; he harasses me at home and work, until I am forced to ask someone from human resources to intervene.

I am too thin, from the stress, and I have terrible, terrible allergies to everything blooming in Florida. West Palm Beach is very pretty, but doesn't feel like the ideal place to be young and single. I think it would be amazing if I were of retirement age.

I look for a new job as a librarian, but what I really want is a complete change of scenery. I'm a bit confused about what I want to do with my library and information science background, and I have always wanted to join the Peace Corps. I even applied once, right out of college. I received an assignment in West Africa, but I turned it down and moved to Los Angeles to be with my then boyfriend.

In 1997, after eighteen months of muddling along in my job at the newspaper library in Florida, I apply again to join the Peace Corps. After watching my outlook go up and down here, I think I want a slower pace of life, a more meaningful purpose, and a place to cultivate inner calm.

Becoming immersed in a totally different culture had helped me once before. When I was nineteen and in undergraduate school in Minnesota, I chose to study abroad in India. The program focused on Buddhism and Buddhist meditation. I figured at the time that the slower pace of life in Bodh Gaya, India, and learning meditation would help me calm down. I was right; I effectively self-treated emotional troubles for a semester. Now I hope to do it again, only for a longer period of time, and I relish the idea of doing truly meaningful work.

The Peace Corps accepts me, and with more excitement than apprehension, I take off for my two-year adventure on a tiny coral island in the Central Pacific.

CHAPTER ONE

It takes a long time to hear back from the Peace Corps once I apply, to see whether I have been accepted or not. On the Peace Corps application, you can select a region of the world to go to, but I choose to leave this line blank, staying open to what might turn out to be a very interesting opportunity.

The letter finally comes, telling me I've been accepted and assigned to the Republic of Kiribati. I have never heard of the place before and have to look it up on the map.

The Republic of Kiribati (pronounced Keer-ee-bahs) is a chain of islands in the Central Pacific basin. Kiribati is right where the equator meets the International Date Line, southwest of Hawaii, and north of Fiji. The thirty-three islands of the Gilbert, Phoenix, and Line islands chains make up this country. Most are coral atolls. Atolls are sunken volcanoes. The *Micronesia Handbook* states, "Legend tells that the god Nareau picked flowers from the ancestral tree and threw them north of Samoa to create the islands of Tarawa, Beru, and Tabiteuea. These islands and thirty others now compose the independent Republic of Kiribati." People in Kiribati speak the Kiribati language, which is its own language, though it has many similar words to other Micronesian languages.

After training, I'm to be stationed on Marakei atoll, one of the Gilbert Islands, where my assignment is to train villagers in health education. Though I am older than many Peace Corps volunteers, there are men and women in my volunteer group who are well into their sixties, and a few in their forties.

Before leaving the States, I say goodbye to family and friends, and my job, send out a mass letter to friends all over the States letting them know where I'm going, what I'll be doing, and what my mailing address will be. Most of my friends are supportive. My parents are concerned that going into the Peace Corps is not "financially responsible," even though Peace Corps does give volunteers a modest monthly stipend while one is volunteering, and a similar stipend in a lump sum at the completion of two years.

My plan is to finish work in late September 1997, travel to New Orleans, Minnesota, and Los Angeles to visit family and friends, and then fly to San Francisco to meet my group of other Peace Corps volunteers, with whom I will journey on to Kiribati to begin new adventures. In my group, there are rural health education volunteers, of which I am a part, and education volunteers, who will be assigned to primary schools and junior secondary schools. All of us will be assigned to the outer islands.

The Peace Corps Volunteer Assignment Description states,

> The Ministry of Environment and Social Development (MESD) has asked Peace Corps to help

improve health education and promotion in the rural communities. Your objective is to work under the supervision of the Island Clerk to help Island Community workers (ICW) and Women Interest Workers (WIW) learn and use better ways of delivering health education and promotion activities to women and youth and the outer island communities as a whole. You will be assigned to an outer island where you will work with groups and individuals from all of the interested villages on that particular island. You will conduct meetings and training workshops with women and youth on health-related issues. Training packages for these meetings and trainings will be made available to you during your pre-service training.

Before going to Marakei, I undergo a three-month training program that includes staying with host families in the capital of Tarawa, and on the outer islands of Abemama and Aranuka. Throughout the cultural, language, and technical training, I learn so much sometimes my head is overflowing. Never in my life have I seen so many stars or beautiful sunsets or such blue lagoons. The training and language lessons are hard, but after a few weeks I start to get a grasp on what role I might play as a health education volunteer. Running in the mornings during training, I clock time, not distance. It is so hot it takes me a week to be able to run twenty minutes a day. I think of the idea of culture shock somewhere around the time the pigs and chickens outside the bathing area wander into the *roki* (latrine) while I have dysentery.

During training, I wonder if I will ever get used to being here? Will I adjust to taking bucket baths? Will I ever get used to the pit latrine? Will I ever be able to bike long distances in a skirt regularly, as women mostly wear skirts in Kiribati? Throughout training, I am woken up repeatedly at 1:30 a.m. by a chorus of howling, mangy dogs. Once they quiet, the roosters start crowing. Then my neighbors' pigs squeal, and finally I fall asleep, only to be awakened again at six by roosters and men singing songs as they perform the ritual of cutting toddy. They bind and cut a spathe and then collect the sap that accumulates in the morning and at night, by tying bottles to the part of the tree where the sap comes out. Roosters crow all the time.

I want to do this and be successful with it and this next chapter in life. I am a little occupied thinking about what island I'll be placed on and what my house will look like. It is during this training that I think I want to be stationed on the island of Marakei, but I am determined to have a good experience wherever I go.

As a part of this training, myself and two other trainees, one other health volunteer, and one for education are sent to Abemama Island to stay with Susan, an education volunteer, for a week. Susan has four structures for her house, including a cook house, *roki* (toilet and bathing area), her main house with her bed, and a *buia*, her open-air structure with a thatch roof that is more like a porch to sit on, sleep on, or eat on.

Susan tells Lisa, Jean, and me that at night she locks the door for the night. "I don't like to go out to the *roki* after dark, so I pee on the coral rocks in the corners of my house, where there are no mats on the floor." So we assume it's fine to do this, though a little strange.

We are woken that night by the howling dogs. After this ends, the roosters start in with their crowing. Lisa gets up to pee by the door, and I realize I need to pee too. Unlocking the door and tripping to the *roki* in the dark is too much effort, so I pee by the door too. When the stench starts in, I wonder if Susan got used to the smell of pee roasting in equatorial heat. I do not smell this in homes of I-Kiribati people.

Then Lisa starts writing in her journal; her flashlight is on, and I can't find my earplugs. "Wow," I think: local people sleep through all of this. Sleeping on a thin woven mat made of pandanus tree leaves is also an adjustment. I definitely think I'll need my thermarest, an inflatable camping mattress I brought with me to Kiribati but left in Tarawa at the Peace Corps dorm storage, when I'm permanently stationed at my eventual island site.

One of my fellow volunteers puts it plainly: It probably wouldn't be the Peace Corps if everything were real cushy. I wish that I had thought more about all the stuff I would actually need and brought more of it. But then, we were limited in baggage, and one can only ship so much stuff in the mail. The list they sent us of what to bring seems inane now that I'm "in country" and see what's really needed.

For instance, they told us to bring long skirts, because women only wear skirts. So, I bought cheap skirts. Problem is, some of them are straight skirts, which you can't sit in cross-legged in a *maneaba* (longhouse). So I'm learning to adjust. The bucket bathing too…it's not as nice as a shower, but it *is* actually refreshing after sweating so much in the heat.

"This experience feels very far away from home, both physically and metaphorically," I share with my friend Kayla, another Peace Corps health educator in training with me. "Yes," she agrees, "it certainly does." It's not that I didn't know I would be living in a stick house. They told us this ahead of time. It's just that it's actually dawning on me that

I'll be living in a stick house for two years. Training itself is discombobulating and draining, and I need to adjust. The Peace Corps staff running the training keep us busy from morning to night, and then time with our host family takes up the rest of the day. There is little time to oneself, which I am used to having more of. The good thing is that training is only for a few months.

During Peace Corps training, I wish I had more space because living in a one-room structure with seven people is not something I'm used to. On top of that, I feel like the obnoxious American because my host family back on Tarawa, in their quest to be nice, has given me the one bed they have, despite my cries that I don't need it and would be perfectly happy on my thermarest I've hauled from the States. I am afraid of putting them out, but they say they insist they want me to be happy with the arrangement.

There is lack of privacy and lack of control over my own diet. I realize I'm going to have to ask one of the language teachers how to say that I like certain foods, and that others upset my stomach. There is never enough time to myself to catch my breath in training, but I know this will change when I get to my permanent site. I can feel my personality being squished and I'm unhappy this bothers me so much. It is easy during this time to lose sight of the big picture, and get a skewed perspective, since I'm not yet independent on my work site island, nor can I control my living situation. My prayers are that it will be better and easier when I get to "my" island. At times, I wonder "what have I gotten myself into for two years?"

I speak with Traci, one of the health education trainers and a former Peace Corps Kiribati volunteer herself, about this. She tells me to "just make the best of it for this short time. You will have more control over things once you have your own home and are a part of a village. Also remember," she points out, "you'll feel better once you have more control of the language."

Reading the *Kiribati Visitor Handbook* for 1997-1998, I find:

> Welcome. Thank you for considering Kiribati for your holiday. We look forward to welcoming you and hope you will enjoy being with us. We hope you will appreciate the values we consider important, family, hospitality, peace and tranquility, time of conversation and sharing, and time to relax.
>
> We put these values ahead of television (we have none) work (we do work but we have not become slaves to it), and the pressures of modern life. We are proud of our country; it is peaceful, quiet, and safe.

I have dance rehearsals in the *maneaba* (longhouse) with the *unimwane* (the old wise men) pounding on the huge wooden box drums. I don't always have the right amount of rhythm to do *buki* dancing, but all the volunteers in my group have been split into smaller groups to learn traditional Kiribati dances. I am in a group with two fellow health education volunteers and friends, Jane and Maryann. Thankfully, we get a short dance to learn.

Training on Tarawa and the outer islands is ending. I have been assigned to the island of Marakei (mare-uh-kay), which is what I wanted. Marakei is known for good snorkeling, an enclosed lagoon, flying fish, traditional *buki* dancing, and *tabunea* (magic, both black and white). I chose Marakei as my first choice of islands, so this is very good.

Kayla, my fellow volunteer friend, and I walk by the Catholic church near Tarawa Teachers College near the end of training, and she asks, "do you want to see the stained-glass window inside the church?" Upon entering, Kayla decides to light a candle. I say I'll light one and ask for St. Anthony to watch over all the stuff we sent on the ships to "our" islands, though I'm not Catholic.

There are parts of the road on Tarawa that go from the airport at Bonriki to the wharf down at Betio, where you can see from one side of the island to the other. The width is maybe only the distance of an American block across. I sit in buses in Tarawa and stare out beyond the narrow strip of island. The view from one window is the lagoon and the view from the other is the ocean. You can see coconut trees on little islets not too far offshore.

In the post-training week after swearing in as a volunteer, before shipping out, I go to pick up two large metal basins for water, bathing, and washing that will be shipped out to my site on Marakei. I also pick up a large sheet metal oven that fits directly over the top of the burners on the small kerosene stove I bought, and a pan from the Tarawa Metalworks shop, across town from where the volunteers stay in the Peace Corps dormitory. I place the order for my bike, a green Schwinn roadster, to be shipped out later from the one bike shop on Tarawa.

I haul all this stuff, sans bicycle, back on a minivan-style bus with umpteen other squished souls vying for seat room. The bus comfortably seats fifteen, but there are twenty-four on it along with my metal goods and me. Cruising along at breakneck speed on bush roads in between the ocean and lagoon is a bit chaotic. This particular bus has no door, so more kids decide to climb on and hang on for dear life in the open doorway, while the techno-music blares from a cassette player at hearing-loss decibels.

Navigating getting out of the bus with all my metal

goods, while trying to make sure my *lava lava*, a piece of fabric wrapped around oneself like a sarong, doesn't fall off is a challenge. I can't help but laugh when, as the bus zips away, I am left standing on the side of the road, clenching the fabric of my *lava lava* and my loot, still able to hear the bus music blaring and kids singing along to, "*I'm a Barbie girl in a Barbie world. Ride the plastic. It's fantastic. You can brush my hair, undress me everywhere. Imagination. That's your creation. Come on, Barbie, let's go party.*"

CHAPTER TWO

In January 1998 I'm sworn in as a Peace Corps volunteer. I learn another traditional *buki* dance to perform with two other female volunteers. We perform for the president of the country, Teburoro Tito, his wife, Madame Keina, and assembled dignitaries. I wear a huge pandanus leaf skirt and other traditional dance costume regalia on my head, arms, and chest. Though I am not very good, I understand how many stories of the Kiribati people get told through song and dance, even from the little I have just learned.

Between swearing-in and flying out to Marakei, I must ship my kerosene stove, kettle, basins, and all those supplies I'd purchased to take out to my posting. Everything is shipped from Tarawa to Marakei on boats. Peace Corps has given us a stipend to buy all the things we'll need for setting up a home at our new posts. I also buy tinned food that the shops will ship out to my site for me. The bicycle, which will be my main transport, will also be shipped out on a boat.

I fly to Marakei island: Look at the pin dot just slightly

northeast of Tarawa on a map. That's Marakei island, where I will be for two years. Everything that can't fit on a small prop plane has to be shipped from Tarawa to each of the country's outer islands, such as Marakei, on the small cargo boats that do inter-island freight.

Flying into Marakei from Tarawa for the first time, on the small prop plane, I see a perfect pear shape with the lagoon in the middle, brilliant blues and greens, with millions of coconut trees. I see a dirt strip runway at the northern part of the island, and people, bicycles, and luggage made out of nylon yellow rice bags standing by the small concrete house that serves as the airport. After being greeted by the island's public health nurse, Mareko, and his wife, Emeri, and traveling around the island, I am taken to the island guest house, since my house is still being finished.

My house on Marakei, which the villagers have made me, has walls made of the mid-ribs of the coconut tree, lashed together with rope made from the inner webbing of the coconut. The beams are coconut tree trunks. There is a point built into the corners of thatch in my roof that is cut a certain way (down) to, I'm told, ward off spells or magic that would cause the home's inhabitants to have stomach troubles. My house appears very sturdy, though you could cut the rope holding the walls together with a butter knife. I lock my door with a simple cable bicycle lock hooked through the slats. I hang things around and put maps of the world, pictures, and interesting and inspiring quotes on the walls, all things that came with me from the States. I am able to hang a small portable mirror I bought in the capitol on one of the slats that makes up a wall in my house. If I hop up and down a bit, I can try to see what my whole body looks like.

When Mareko, Emeri, and their extended family first

greeted me at the Marakei airport when, we drove on one of the two flatbed trucks on the atoll counterclockwise around the island, to give the traditional offerings of tobacco to four female statues at four different places on the island. This tradition is in order to "appease" the stone women and assure a good stay for me on Marakei. The statues have names like Nei Rotebenoa or Nei Tongongo, and the legend says that offering them tobacco will allow these two, at least, to see that the traveler on Marakei has a safe trip and fertility. Nei Nantekimeme, one of the other *bangotas*, or stationary stone women, carries the ability to have sweet (as opposed to salty) drinking water from the ocean near where she resides.

Within a few weeks, it becomes known via the ship captains coming to deliver cargo, that all the goods I purchased in Tarawa, except for my bike and stove, went overboard when one of the smaller dinghy type boats transporting said cargo off the bigger ship bound for Marakei, capsized. That'll teach me I shouldn't be lighting a candle to St. Anthony or reciting, "St. Anthony, St. Anthony, please look around, something's been lost and needs to be found" when it's not my religion.

There are two other Peace Corps volunteers also on Marakei. Yeekyong and Brigitte are both education volunteers working in elementary schools and junior secondary schools, teaching English. We will see each other at *botakis*, festival type parties that take place in the longhouse, but not many other places.

Now on Marakei, I wake to the sounds of the ocean waves and my neighbor, Wiriam, singing songs while cutting toddy for his family. I hear him singing to his coconut tree while he binds and cuts a new spathe every morning and every night, hanging an empty bottle from the spathe, and collecting the sweet sap that drips out. The toddy is added to the family's drinking water, or poured over rice. While I was in training, I couldn't get used to the taste, but now I seem to have adjusted. Toddy is high in vitamin A, and many people here are vitamin A deficient. It's one of the few sources of vitamin A villagers routinely consume in their diet, but not everyone drinks enough to counteract deficiencies. Wiriam's toddy-cutting tree has big machete chunks taken out of the bark, to carve out steps for him to use to climb up high.

I have only been on Marakei a week when I am told by island council workers and a female teacher about six men to "be careful" of. Six on an island of 2500 people. They are rapists, perverts, or psychotics, according to the descriptions I am given. The women are blasé about telling me this: "Oh yes, and him, he goes around raping people." They tell me to be careful of any men who come to my house after drinking, as alcoholism and drinking sour toddy are quite common. The alcohol is made by letting the fresh toddy ferment. The latter is something I am familiar with from training. I'm cautioned not to go biking far away by myself. I should go with someone.

Mareko goes out with me to various health education trainings when I first arrive on Marakei. After that, he has some student nurses who accompany me during their short stay on the island, as part of their nursing school coursework. Two women named Tien and Mere, both nursing students, are very helpful and glad to get health education experience in the villages. I help them fill their requirements, and they help me translate my sessions, and make posters and props in Kiribati language.

Mareko is too busy to accompany me every time I go to villages outside Rawannawi, the Marakei government headquarters and main village. The island project officer is too busy as well. My other possible counterpart, the women's interest worker, is on maternity leave, to be followed by annual leave, and not to return for the entire year of 1998. Mareko, the members of the Island Council, and the policeman all think I can go to some of the closer villages by myself, but going *buokonikai* (through the bush to more distant villages) is deemed not safe.

Not wanting to put up a fuss over a local custom, I let it be. They want me to be accompanied. It is not just the language barrier. My language is getting much better, though people still need some help understanding my accent and grammar. If I can take the *repe repe* (reh-pay, reh-pay, the motorbike so named because of the coughing stutter sound the engine makes when it starts up), then people will not worry about me, though they hint it's hardly ever available. When I do get the *repe repe*, I tie my *lava lava* on tight, and go 17 miles per hour, the maximum speed, on the benzene-fueled Yamaha. It's more like a moped. Mareko and Emeri also take me around Marakei island and introduce me to the *neeti n te kaawa* (village nurses) and other village welfare group leaders.

Peace Corps wants new volunteers to conduct a "needs assessment" for health education and promotion activities on Marakei. This means I ask and survey and cajole people in various informal and formal ways to tell me what types of health education and health-related activities they need. In reality, I feel they tell me what they think I want to hear. I am not certain I will ever hear what they *really* want to tell me. Not many people speak English to me, and Mareko tries to get me to converse only in Kiribati as well. This is okay, although mildly frustrating, as I am trying to get better at the Kiribati language. Sometimes it is just lonely.

The women in my *makoro* (section of a village) all tell me they want to build more wells and latrines, but those who already have latrines still use the beach to defecate. They do this because they don't like the idea that the waste is close to their house (even though they "flush" by pouring water down the pit latrine hole), and because they believe the ocean waves carry the waste far away. Both cultural reasons are understandable to me. The nurses want help with health education and the agriculture guy wants seeds for gardens.

Itabera and Baraniko, friends of Mareko and Emeri, have been helping me with my Kiribati language. This is hard, and it's helping me improve. She is a preschool teacher and they have had contact with many of the English-speaking Mormon missionaries who have come in the past. There is also a motivation to learn the I-Kiribati language for social reasons. It is the way to become a part of the community, to make friends with the single girls my age or younger, to do my actual job better, and to joke around with neighbors and villagers.

I can barely go eighteen meters out of my house without hearing, "Nei Amy, *ko naera?*" (Miss Amy, where are you going?) from someone. In a typical day, I hear "*ko naera, ko naera, ko naera?*" every time I go anywhere. If I pass a village on my bike, I hear it called out from *buias,* the open air thatch structures near people's homes, everywhere. I also hear, "Nei Amy, *motirawa.*" (Miss Amy, come rest and talk with us here.) If I had a dime for every time I heard *motirawa*, I'd be rich, and if I actually *motirawa'd* with everyone who asked me to, I would never get anywhere or get anything done. My days here are often planned according to the heat, *botakis* (festivals), and village *maneaba* (longhouse) gatherings. Cooking and handwashing clothes both take a long time, but there is nothing to really rush off to here anyway.

My attitude has changed too. I realize dirt washes off easily and I look forward to my two bucket baths a day. Dip and pour, dip and pour. People here are very concerned about cleanliness and keeping their land tidy; they either "landscape" with coral from the ocean, or constantly sweep the dirt around their homes to control the dust by keeping the earth packed down.

Villagers on Marakei are very generous and not long after I arrive, the women make and give me four *tibutas* (see-boo-tuhs), smocked women's blouses with my name embroidered on the chest. Neighbors teach me how to cook different kinds of fish and local foods, and I learn to borrow fire from someone else's cook fire to light my own (when I don't cook over my stove) by carrying a burning branch or pandanus leaf like a torch across the dirt road back to my house.

After a few months, I begin to get more used to life here. People who teach preschoolers that roosters only crow at dawn have apparently never lived in an area with lots of roosters. I'm awakened by many, at many different hours, so have taken to using the earplugs I brought from the States but thought I would never need.

In the U.S., one can go weeks without seeing their neighbors, yet here I see the same people over and over again. My neighbors help me drag a *buia* from near the pig pen all the way up towards my house. My *buia* is like an open-air porch. The kids and fathers also go to the beach thirty feet away and haul lots of white coral to scatter around by my water pump and around the front of the yard for coral landscaping. They tell me, "You don't have a husband or family to do this for you here." Being single is looked at as strange here, especially if you don't have family with whom to stay.

It's hot, so sometimes I just sit in the evening with my door open and swing in the hammock I've hung between two wooden beams near my entryway. It's consistently in the high eighties with 80 percent humidity. Sometimes I get so hot and sweaty during the day that I'm exhausted after biking only three villages away, probably just a few kilometers.

CHAPTER THREE

Since Mareko cannot always accompany me to health education sessions, and the student nurses are leaving, and I need to still go biking with someone else, I have to start thinking of whom to ask for help. Mareko and his wife, Emeri, think they know the perfect person for the job: Tuutana, who is a distant relative of theirs. Their families are close, and she calls Emeri "Auntie."

Tuutana is short and a bit stocky, with very long black hair held up in plastic combs or terry-cloth binders. Emeri asks Tuutana's parents if Tuutana can accompany me to Antai village and they say yes. Tuutana is looked at by her family as very independent-minded and she likes to do things with her male cousins more often than with her sisters. Though no one seems thrilled about two "girls" going off on bicycles to Antai (it would be safer and better culturally if we were two girls with a man or an older boy), this is seen as the solution for now; in villagers' eyes, it beats letting me go off on my own.

Tuutana, who is nineteen, has finished school, but she

hasn't passed the next test to go on in school in the Tarawa/Kiribati European educational model. She has returned to Marakei from her schooling in Tarawa. She moves back into Anterea and Eritabeta's house. They are her father's brother and his wife, but she has been living with them since before her *babako* (adopted grandmother) and the grandmother's husband moved to New Zealand ten years earlier. To Tuutana, both Anterea and Eritabeta are her parents. She has little contact with her biological father. Anterea is a teacher at one of the primary schools in Rawannawi village, but he has been a member of the Kiribati parliament in the past, representing Marakei. Tuutana connects with family and old friends from Marakei after being on other islands for school for the last few years. She hangs out with and helps Eritabeta with household chores and, in her spare time, starts to practice with the girls' soccer team in Rawannawi village.

The first time I meet Tuutana, she's like a turtle, occasionally sticking her head out of her shell to look at me or ask a question. Otherwise, it's straight ahead quiet biking on the road or Anoteh the two of us travel to get to the village of Antai. She isn't scared of *I-Matangs* (white people) and in fact has met many. But I am definitely the first white woman in her age range whom she has met and conversed with, beyond perfunctory hellos and welcomes she has grown up doing when introduced to foreigners. This time, she's being asked to accompany the new Peace Corps volunteer, me, to a health session I am teaching.

On the bike ride to Antai, Tuutana and I ride in silence. She seems overly cautious around me, and gives me monosyllabic answers to my questions, like *"eng"* (yes) or *"akea"* (no). I see her laughing and joking with her friends just before we leave, so I know she's not always shy. At Antai village, she sits on her bike seat like a mute bump on a log and refuses to go into the *maneaba*, or village longhouse. She says she's not giving the presentation with the village nurse and me, which is true, and that she'll wait on a *buia*, outside the *maneaba*, with some of her acquaintances.

She has a sort of stubborn and immature streak because once she is finally requested to come into the *maneaba* by some male village elders, she sucks it up and enters, mumbling, "*I maama, ao iai naba, tiaki ngai te I-Matang.*" ("I'm shy, and besides I'm not the white girl.") There are twenty-four village women from Antai for the session on water and hygiene, conducted because two children have died in neighboring villages recently from diarrhea-induced dehydration caused by lack of clean water. The *Kamwengaraoi*, or village welfare group, decides to start inspecting the village homes to make sure people are boiling their water.

Biking back from Antai with Tuutana that first day, we still ride in silence, but there seems to be less attitude. She includes me in a conversation with her cousin in the village, just before we head back to Rawannawi. I ask if she'll come with me to future health sessions and she doesn't say no, which I take as a partial yes.

Tuutana and I end up biking to different villages every week. We go to Tekarakan and Temotu villages, and she goes with me to visit some of the village nurses. She tells me, "*I maku teutana te taetae.*" ("I'm a little scared of speaking the language," meaning the English.) But between my so-so Kiribati and her so-so English, we're off and running. Eventually, she tells me about not passing the test to go on in school in the their education system, and that is why she has returned to Marakei. Anterea and Eritabeta have really been her parents for the last ten years, "since my *babako* went to Auckland," she tells me. Tuutana, when I ask about her biological family, says, "I have *teutana* (little) contact with my father, but he lives in Rawannawi village," where she and I both live. "My biological mother died when my younger sister, Tobia, and I were toddlers. We have an older sister as well; she lives on the nearby island of Abaiang."

I find myself a bit homesick. I miss "instant gratitude"--turning a tap for water, zapping food in a microwave, light switches, and showers. But when I haul my water in buckets so I can bathe, wash my clothes by hand, wash my dishes, and flush the latrine, I talk to my neighbors, island council workers and policemen, and their families. While pumping my water and hanging my clothes on the line to dry, I ask people "How do I make *tari* (salted fish)?" or I invite the children, "Come play dominoes with me." I always get friendly and helpful replies. I realize everything is a trade-off. I have taken to running every morning as the sun rises over the ocean and I watch it set over a blue lagoon every night. This is very grounding. Work is good, but a bit frustrating. Sometimes I wish some counterpart or local leader would take me under his or her wing a bit more, the way the school teachers do with the Peace Corps education volunteers.

I don't see much of Brigitte or Yeekyong. Our jobs are so different, and they are mostly confined to their school compounds. I see them at a few different *botakis* that we are all invited to. I have more fun with Tuutana than with them, which I find interesting, since they and I are from the same country.

CHAPTER FOUR

People live off the land here. One can eat fish and homegrown bok choy or Brazilian spinach, breadfruit, pandanus fruit, and *bwabwai* (giant swamp taro) here all the time. What villagers don't get from the sea or land, they buy at the small, locally owned stores. I even know who bakes the buns and donuts in the stores, which are mostly stocked with flour, sugar, rice, and a small selection of tinned food. In Tarawa, you can get canned cheese with Arabic lettering and the Kraft logo on it. It tastes good, but I wonder if my standards have changed, since it's kind of like Velveeta, but white. There is also Pablo brand instant coffee, Ox & Palm canned corned beef, and MaLing Curried Chicken in the small stores on Marakei.

You can eat fish and coconut and breadfruit and edible leaves and pandanus and *bwabwai* forever, and sometimes it feels I will be doing this. Many times, I am given way too much food to be consumed by one person, by my kind neighbors or other helpful villagers. It would be considered rude to refuse or admit you don't want it, and no one wants to share my tons of gifted rice and fish and taro. As there's no refrigeration, I give it to my pet pig, WilburTwo.

I got a pig in the first place to give food to, and to eventually give away to a *botaki* of some of my adopted family or friends later on. Most everyone here has pigs. In fact, WilburTwo is my second pig. The first pig, Wilbur, was under my *buia*, and tied to one of the legs of the *buia*, but then his leg got sore and I didn't want him to end up like some of the neighbors' three-legged pigs. The three-legged pigs get like that after one leg falls off at the infected part, where the rope tying them up cuts into them.

My neighbors and I built that first Wilbur a pen, and then he died of a twisted gut. At least, that's what the agricultural worker on the island told me, though there was no way to confirm it. He got renamed WilburOne posthumously. My neighbor buried him for me under a coconut tree by the ocean and the tree grew well, though a few months later I could have sworn I saw and smelled a bloated pig carcass out on the rocks at low tide. It could have been someone else's pig, or perhaps one of the mangy dogs roaming around unearthed old WilburOne for grub.

My friend Beatirike's husband, TeNikora, has some new piglets and he gifts me one that I name WilburTwo. No one on Marakei gets the *Charlotte's Web* reference, but then it isn't like I am in the habit of calling my pig anyway. In any case, I am determined not to have my second pig go bad on me. I talk to Nei Teretia, the policeman's wife, who lives right next to me. She tells me, "Nei Amy, take the new piglet and cover his fur with *te ba* (coconut oil), and then stick him under your armpit and go into the ocean with him, so he will get to know your smell and your sound." So I do this, and it seems to work.

WilburTwo is a tiny piglet when I do this, about small

puppy size, but he whines a big pig whine when I go into the ocean with him. Then, when I take him out of the ocean, he seems mad. But after that, every time I come home from being out in one of the villages, he seems to know it's me and he whines for his food or more water. I think WilburTwo whines when I come home because he smells me. My neighbors confirm this by saying, "He doesn't whine when you're not there during the daytime."

WilburTwo eats all the excess food and taro I'm given and can't consume. He often eats these large quantities at night when it's dark, after I come home with food gifts. I don't want the neighbors who gave me a family supper for four to see my pig enjoying it.

After a few months the policeman, Waoreta, and his family share with me more Kiribati knowledge about pig growth. This pig wisdom, whether I believe it or not, is supposed to help WilburTwo grow up to be a big pig for a big *botaki*. Pigs are raised to be eaten at big *botakis*. You gauge the size or importance of the *botaki* by the number of pigs killed for the meal. At this point I am not thinking of what I will do with WilburTwo when I leave Marakei; I just want him to grow. Waoreta's wife, Taua, opens WilburTwo's mouth and Waoreta takes a small knife to cut a tiny "v" shape in the roof of the pig's mouth. "If he has a small cut there, he'll eat more trying to rub that cut with food," Waoreta explains, and I see that WilburTwo seems to eat much more after that.

You can feed a pig almost anything, but I am told old fish and guts and blood have to be cooked first so the pig doesn't get sick. And you also can never give him onions or onionskin. "Pigs die from onions," I'm warned. My pig has separate feeders for water and for food. The feeders are made from big black truck tires that are cut open sideways to make troughs for the food and water. I try to keep the feeders clean, and to bury his waste, or at least to shovel enough dirt over it so he doesn't sit in the pen with his own feces.

After losing WilburOne, I try to be very careful about WilburTwo's health. Ten Biribo, the island's agricultural officer, came and gave WilburTwo shots one time when he spent the day lying in the mud all day and not eating or drinking. I don't know what he gave him in the shots, or what WilburTwo even had. When Waoreta and Taua transfer to another island, the other Marakei policeman, TeRui, and his wife, Teria, start answering my pig questions.

CHAPTER FIVE

Eritabeta calls Tuutana a tomboy, and she seems to act accordingly. In her free time, if not with me or other friends, she is always off playing soccer. As a rule, Tuutana won't wear *lava lavas* (sarongs) or skirts, except if necessary for a church service; she changes into a skirt or *lava lava* for the duration of the service, then quickly changes back to long shorts as soon as church is over. I think she can get away with this because she's not being scrutinized as the foreigner (like I am), and she's not married yet. Once she gets married, it looks to me like it's skirts or *lava lavas* for her on Marakei.

As a foreigner, I have two pair of shorts, both down to below my knees, and I only get to wear them around my house and the surrounding area. Many men here have images of morally and sexually loose Western women that maybe they pick up when generator-powered videos are shown in the villages. It's ironic, because I've never worn such long skirts in my life. The only time I see my own thighs is in the latrine, and it's a big cultural taboo to "flash" your thighs when you sit down cross-legged in the *maneaba*. Women generally don't show their thighs to anyone but their husbands from what I gather. I concentrate hard when I sit down in my long skirts, bunching up the fabric in one hand next to my leg, while dropping and quickly tucking my legs underneath me.

Since finishing school, Tuutana has spent time reconnecting with family and old friends from Marakei. She introduces me to Teretia and Marenuea, and other "young women," which basically means other unmarried women to hang out with. Young just means unmarried in this case, but it could be any age under forty.

A few months after our first ride to Antai, I borrow the island council *repe repe*, and Tuutana and I take off to Bainuna village to tell them about a prenatal health care session the following week. On the way, she tells me about her cousin, Akineti, raised as an older sister to her.

"Amy, Akineti fell in love with a man whose family didn't like her. He and Akineti were told they couldn't marry, and shortly thereafter they hung themselves from coconut trees in the bush."

I'm the same age Akineti would have been had she lived, and in some ways, I see that Tuutana treats me as an *I Matang*, a foreigner, older sister. In looking at old family photos at Anterea and Eritabeta's house, I see pictures of Akineti and Tuutana as kids playing together in Tarawa shortly after Tuutana's grandmother moved to New Zealand.

Not too long after the trip to Bainuna, where she tells me about her cousin Akineti's suicide, Tuutana and I bike to the villages of Tekarakan and Temotu, where I have to visit some village nurses. Mareko and Emeri took me around the island when I first arrived and introduced me to the *neeti n te kaawa* (village nurses) and other village welfare group leaders I would need to know. Upon Tuutana's and my return to Rawannawi, Emeri and Mareko call to us on the road to *"motirawa"* (have a rest). Their house is situated on a large plot of land that includes the main Marakei health clinic. The clinic is a small building with open windows, a permanently ajar door, a small solar-powered refrigerator for vaccines that goes out of commission every time it rains, and boxes and boxes of medicines stamped "Donated by the World Health Organization."

Ten Bauro, Mareko and Emeri's relative, has just arrived on the plane. They want to introduce him to Tuutana and me. He's visiting after a few years overseas on a German ship, where he works as a seaman. One of the ways Kiribati people make money is for the men to pass the test to be seamen on German or Japanese fishing vessels or cargo ships. These are large commercial vessels, and the men go away to work on them for a few years at a time. Their families can receive the seaman's remittances back home through wire transfer to the bank in Tarawa.

Bauro is in his late twenties and says he's been having fun living on the ship and exploring bars and women at different ports. He hangs around Emeri and Mareko's house for almost four months, and occasionally bikes different places with Tuutana and me. I think he's a little bit of what the Kiribati call *"kaintiroaki"* (show off or boasting), but I don't say anything. Tuutana thinks he's worldly and funny. "He's good for the *kakibotu*, for taking away the boredom," she says, and I can see that talking to him while handwashing bucket after bucket of dirty clothes of family laundry or other daily chores would liven up doing said chores.

Bauro and Tuutana hang out at her family's house a lot, and she just laughs and sort of raises her eyebrows in the

Kiribati affirmative way when I ask her if they're dating. Their relationship is cautiously watched, but not talked about. He's only off his ship for a few months' vacation and then he ships out again. He has a drinking problem, witnessed by his spending a part of everyday drunk, but he is generally nice, and she seems to be having fun with him.

People don't date in Kiribati. They either *"biri aki nako"*; this means elope, and roughly translates as run, don't go... as in don't go have an official wedding; or they go to the church and have an actual service. Once a girl or a woman has slept with someone, she's married to that person or she's damaged goods. And since Marakei is an island of only 2500, people know most things going on in the village. In addition, most people are related to each other in some way.

Emeri and Mareko's daughter, Kamoia, has her fourth birthday *botaki*. There is a large party with all their family and friends. Food comes in on the plane from Tarawa with friends, such as frozen hot dogs and chicken breasts. Tuutana and I help out with the food in the kitchen and baking a cake. We make a salad dressing for the cabbage, which is *rangi ni kangkang* (very delicious), and made with Sunshine brand powdered milk, honey, and a little water.

I love fish now, whether raw, salted, sautéed, boiled, steeped in coconut milk, curried, or plain. I eat octopus tentacles for dinner sometimes. The outside purplish/brownish tentacle suction cup part, after being cooked, is gross to me. It's sort of a slippery texture, but the meat inside is white, tender, and very good. It's soft because the women beat it with a stick before they cook it to tenderize it. The men catch them in their holes with long hook-type metal rods, which they stick down in the holes to drive the octopi out of their hiding places in the ocean.

I also eat a lot of breadfruit. Breadfruit trees have many

varieties and remind me of Mother Earth. They're big and they flourish, spilling fruit that's overripe and letting you poke off all the rest with long, long sticks fashioned with a knife on the end. My neighbor, T'Antarea, uses a stick like this to spear off almost ripe breadfruit. Breadfruit are sliced and pan fried, boiled, or made into breadfruit soup, or if very ripe, eaten fresh off the tree. Eritabeta, Tuutana's mother, cooks some form of breadfruit almost every day.

At *botakis,* or celebratory events in the *maneaba,* such as Kamoia's fourth birthday, women wave palm fronds over food to scatter the flies, or they throw stones when the dogs or cats get too close. Food is often cooked early in the morning for late afternoon or evening botakis; it sits in basins or Tupperware containers, which they buy in stores in Tarawa, under cloth *lava lavas.* There is no refrigeration of items here, so I know just have to be careful, but may still get sick. Knowing that, for example, sometimes people rinse off their dirty hands in the dirty dish water basin, then put dishes in there to clean them off later on and don't change that water often enough. This is one simple example, but I see that teaching basic public health education also makes me aware of simple public health challenges like handwashing and food/dishes. I didn't realize I'd be getting a crash course in some vector control topics, but I am.

Nevertheless, I still take chances. I eat *oraora* (raw fish), which is extremely tasty, though one can get sick. I do get sick one day from fish poisoning from a barracuda, along with two other people from Tuutana's family. It is a massively large fish, bigger than some of the huge sharks the men sometimes haul in from their fishing expeditions. At first, I feel achy, and then I can't move my legs. I feel sluggish for two days, until the toxins leave my system. Despite this, I still take chances and eat the different types of fish and food offered to me.

The reality of this new health education program is that people here on Marakei are not exactly certain what to do with me. It's a new program, so we all wonder: Do I work only with the public health nurses, village nurses, island council workers, women's interest worker, village welfare groups? Or do I alternate between all of them? It is hard to find a place, but the beauty is that I get to meet such different and interesting villagers from various backgrounds this way, rather than being pegged to one school or main government office, where that entity "takes care of the volunteer," so to speak. This adds to a little confusion of those on the island a bit, but we find ways to make it work. Though I do have some days where I feel confused, and a bit homesick, my initial months on Marakei are a welcome respite from the negative job in Florida. The constant sense of newness and adventure here, combined with the slower pace of life, keep my mind and outlook on an even keel.

I do feel a tad dismayed by how I look when I catch a glimpse of myself. I mostly wear *tibuta* blouses and funky-colored long skirts. *Tibutas* are cool and loose, and I see that they make my body look like a woman in maternity garb. I've been sweating so much I've got zits galore from the heat, and the Peace Corps medical officer, much happier to treat acne than dengue fever, doles out sulfa soap like it's Ivory. In the first few months, I always wear my glasses, afraid to try out my contact lenses, with all the dust and dirt that's a part of everyday life here. My long, dark hair is either up in a ponytail, or held up with a Kiribati comb. Kiribati hair combs are made from PVC pipe by prisoners in the prison on Tarawa and they have elaborate designs carved into them. The older women I meet sometimes also have hair combs made from discarded metal parts of small airplanes.

My Kiribati is improving because people don't speak English to me, though sometimes if I ask Mareko how to translate an English phrase, he'll humor me and let me know. The language issue is harder at the *botakis*, the big festivals or parties in the *maneaba*, where there are lots of long Kiribati speeches. I often zone out during the speeches, and one time I get fined for not paying attention. This means that I owe the village *maneaba* five Australian dollars, which Kiribati uses for its currency. The fine is for not being respectful enough of the speeches. They apparently asked me a question, and I hadn't even heard they were talking to me, mostly because I probably didn't understand half of what was being said in the speech being given. People get fined randomly all the time for different stuff. It's a way for the *maneaba* to generate money and keep people on their toes.

Botakis are generally fun, though they can take up an entire day. Sitting cross-legged for five hours cramping my legs, and then twisting to generator-powered-blaring-speaker music for another four hours can be exhausting. Sometimes there will be buckets and buckets of lobster or other foods, in addition to these other activities, for eight hours. Being with people who are kind to me and who include me in their village's big events is a nice feeling… one of being part of community.

In training, the volunteers who'd already been here a year said you get used to these long *botakis* after a while, and start looking forward to them, either long or short. I know they're probably right, but they also said my legs, knees, and ankles will get used to sitting in that position for hours on end too, so I'm going to become really limber, or return home arthritic.

Tuutana's adoptive grandmother Karorina, her *babako*, lives in Auckland with her husband and five kids. In the spring of 1998, Karorina's mother Mareta dies and Karorina comes to Marakei from New Zealand for her mother's funeral.

Adoptions, such as an adoptive grandmother, or people who adopt and parent you even though your parents may live elsewhere in the village, like Tuutana with Anterea and Eritabeta, are part of Kiribati culture. The custom of adopting grandchildren carries on from generation to generation.

Karorina talks to Tuutana about eventually coming to New Zealand for work. She has finished school, and what will she do on Marakei? She could live with Karorina's family in Auckland and eventually get work there or get more schooling.

After Karorina returns to Auckland, she and Tuutana talk a few times on the CB/phone. The connection doesn't always work and is patched through radio Kiribati and the Kiribati telephone company. It sounds more like a ham radio than a phone, but Tuutana gets to ask Karorina more questions about New Zealand and what life might be like there. They talk a few times this way, though conversations are a bit guarded since the CB on Marakei is in the island council building and everyone in the government office can hear what's being said.

Despite all the time I spent in language training when I first came to Kiribati, and again here on Marakei, I sometimes can't express myself as well in Kiribati as I'd like. Taking lessons when I first got here with Itabera, and having to work and speak in Kiribati every day have both really helped me. And though I understand most things people say to me, there is still sometimes a language barrier. At times, I find people looking at me, uncertain whether they should tell me that what I just said makes no sense to them, or that I butchered asking for a simple thing in their language. It feels frustrating then.

Tuutana helps me practice speeches and we converse in Kiribati. I learn more from the casual Kiribati conversations I have with her, her family, and others in the village, than from language lessons or the speeches I have to give in Kiribati on various health education topics, mostly because the latter are more scripted.

The Rawannawi girls' soccer team that Tuutana plays on is very good. They play daily, and all the *roro n rikirake*, unmarried people, as well as the rest of the villagers, watch. I find hanging out, watching soccer practice, practicing my Kiribati, and learning about the culture to be more intriguing than my actual job in health education, and find it both interesting and validating when fellow Peace Corps volunteer friends, stationed on other islands, report feeling much the same.

CHAPTER SIX

After half a year, I feel a little less like the new animal at the zoo here. Even the children who used to peer at me through the slats of my house have reduced their daily "stare at the strange white girl" hours. I talk with my neighbors about having another woman stay at my house at night, like we would put up another area for them to sleep in the front room, so I won't be alone if drunk men come to my house in the middle of the night, which has happened a few times. It doesn't occur to me to get a dog, as people don't tend to keep dogs as pets here. The dogs here are more of the wilder and mangier variety than domesticated. Both times drunk men came previously, I loudly yelled, "*Nako!* (go away)" and I heard footsteps running away. The second time, my neighbors came to see what had happened and they saw that someone had cut the wire fence to the garden I've made next to my house, to get access to the side wall of my house, near where I sleep.

Kiribati culture does not allow for much alone time. Family is a big part of the fabric of life here, so people are concerned that I am without my family here. It's good to have kind, loving people who are becoming my adopted family here. Since I've got one foot in one culture and one foot in the other, these kind souls help me feel good and loved here. This helps tremendously while I settle into making a life in Rawannawi village on Marakei island, if even for a few years.

Some of my feeling more at home here begins when I start spending more time with Tuutana and her family and with Mareko and Emeri. Kiribati neighbors, friends, and villagers think it's odd that Peace Corps volunteers have a whole house just to themselves, and I admit it's too much space for one person. I talk to Tuutana about her staying at my house, but she says, "*I maama irouia aomata, bwa I aki maku ke maama iroum*" (I'm shy in front of others and what they would gossip about if I stayed with you, but I'm not shy or scared in front of you). At least we got past her being shy around me, I think to myself. She explains that if they gossip, they'd probably say something like, "That Tuutana thinks she's better than us, because she stays with the *I-Matang*."

Despite being on an island that is very loving and full of community, I do often feel "other," because I am the "other," and I feel alone at times. *Botakis*, family, village, and working the land are all more important priorities here than work or school. And I enjoy these things more than my job anyway. Feeling a lack of personal space during training changed once I got to Marakei, where I finally had some of my own time and could cook for myself or choose to eat with friends and neighbors.

I am being more and more integrated into Tuutana's family. They invite me and include me in everything, and I reciprocate. If I need to go to a faraway village for work,

I see if they need anything from their relatives there, or if they want me to bring something to their relatives. Until now, I've felt like I'm always an honored guest, but that no one knows what to do with me "after the party." At Tuutana's house, it's nice to be expected to help with cooking or the kids, or some such role. I pump and haul water, help cut up the fish or papaya, and teach the very little ones how to eat while still looking out for the bones in their fish.

One Saturday, Tuutana invites me on an outing with her family. We are going on a picnic near one of the ocean picnic spots on the other side of the island. She and I decide to bike to Terokea, where they are picnicking. Terokea is on the far east side of the island, up against the ocean, in between two villages. The family is going on the transport, a flatbed truck hired for the picnic attendees, with the teachers from Nikierere Primary school, but we prefer to go on our own and join them later. On the way, we stop in Norauea village and see some of our mutual friends, and we watch dancing at the Norauea *maneaba* (birthday) *botaki*, a festival to celebrate the building of the Noreaua village longhouse. The villagers ask us to join them in the *maneaba* celebration as guests, but we politely decline, saying we're on our way to a picnic. Tuutana's embarrassed and tells me good-naturedly, "The only reason they even noticed us was because of you. The *I-Matang* stands out in the sea of brown faces." She's right.

We get to the picnic, and there are buckets upon buckets of fresh crab and fish and *bwabwai* and fresh lobster. We eat and take the younger kids out to the ocean at low tide. We look for small seafood in the tide pools to bring back. The little kids spot *te bun, te were, te koikoi*, and we take turns prying open the small shellfish to swallow them down. In the late afternoon, we're all tired. Eritabeta has brought extra mats, and we unroll them on the grassy area and Tuutana and I take a nap with all the girls.

We opt to take the flatbed truck home with the teachers and Eritabeta and Anterea and family. There are so many people that we take the second trip back, sticking our bikes on the flatbed, along with huge bundles of pandanus fruit cut down from trees on land where some of the teachers' families own the property (and therefore those trees.) They will share these with everyone when we return to our village. Pandanus fruit is tri-colored--yellow, orange, and green--and comes in a bunch, all bundled together. Each fruit is the size of an average six-year-old's palm, and you suck the juice out of its fibrous base. The remaining buckets of food, and piles and piles and piles of coconuts fallen, knocked, or cut from trees are also piled on top of the flatbed. Everyone has worked hard to haul these coconuts to where the flatbed truck will pick us up, and they will all work to load them as well. Coconut is necessary for living, and the entire coconut will be used: shells for firewood, the inside "meat" and liquid for cooking and making oil, the webbing for making rope.

After everything is in the truck, Tuutana and I help the younger children up and everyone climbs in and sits on top of the coconuts, delicately balancing the buckets and bikes and people. Unloading coconuts at everyone's house will take as much effort as the gathering did back at the picnic. Trying to make it all fair is a process in and of itself. Everyone wants to make sure they get their fair share. On the way back, we watch out for low-lying coconut tree branches. Everyone ducks and then laughs if we miss spotting one in time and get decked. Grace never having been my forte, I get whacked in the face by a big frond.

These outings and the time I spend with Tuutana in the

villages, or the time I spend with her family, with Eritabeta cooking, or weaving, or just hanging out at mealtimes, show me more about "*te katei*," the Kiribati culture, and I enjoy hanging out with the women who are becoming my family in this place far from home.

CHAPTER SEVEN

Gender roles on Marakei and in Kiribati are sometimes very traditional, but sometimes they surprise me by being the opposite. Take my friend Beatirike, who works in the government station as the island project officer. She earns the money, while her husband, TeNikora (who gifted me WilburTwo), watches their children and does the traditional male jobs of cutting toddy, fishing, and harvesting their family's plot of *bwabwai,* or swamp taro. Women generally do the cooking, the weaving, the sewing and smocking, and the making of thatch. They weave the mats for floors and the mats used for sleeping. They also smock *tibutas*, women's traditional blouses, sew clothes, and embroider elaborate designs on men's "special occasion" *lava lavas*.

It's the women who make and repair the fishing nets for their fathers, husbands, and sons, and who sew and mend the sails for the outrigger canoes. In times past, they would sew together cotton flour bags for sails, but now more and more sails are made out of canvas, plastic tarp, rice bags, or some similar heavy material.

Women usually wear skirts or *lava lavas*, with a *tibuta* on the top. Men usually wear shorts with a *lava lava* over them, or they just wear shorts by themselves, and a t-shirt on top. Younger children, both boys and girls, run around in underpants as soon as they take their school uniforms off. The school uniforms are a white shirt, sewn in a variety of styles, from button down to V-neck, and a pair of royal blue shorts for boys, or a royal blue skirts for girls. Only when the girls get to be pre-teens and self-conscious does the running around in underwear stop; then they start to wear t-shirts. There is a ceremony when a girl first menstruates, where they wear red and stay in a local structure by themselves, learning to make the rope, used for constructing homes, on the canoes, and in toddy cutting, and more. Rope making is traditionally a woman's role. There is also a large *botaki* for the girls at this time in their lives. Clothes that were donated from overseas groups and get sold for a few dollars in Tarawa leave women, men, and kids sometimes wearing shirts that say random things on them in English, without any knowledge of the context, given that they're written in a language that's (more often than not) foreign to the wearer.

Men often fish in handmade outrigger canoes. They make their own canoes from pandanus tree trunks. Pandanus trees look a little like large weeping willows, except that the leaves are long and a couple inches in diameter. It's a big deal when a person finishes making a canoe, and not everyone nor every family has their own, nor the resources or time to build one. Sometimes, extended families will make a canoe as the "family canoe."

When the canoes are out at sea, the men climb out onto the extended outrigger as needed, to balance the canoe. You can see men standing on their boats, and sometimes one more man hanging out to the side over the outrigger to get maximum speed and balance. They seem to manage all this at the same time they haul in big shark, tuna, barracuda, small flying fish, turtles, and more. It's a physical skill, and also requires a lot of knowledge about navigating the ocean in a small vessel.

Canoes are the way people got around the islands and got food for centuries. The Kiribati word for canoe is *wa* or *wana*, which is similar to the same word for canoe in much of Micronesia and even Polynesia. The word for airplane in Kiribati also comes from this: *wanakiba* means flying canoe.

Villagers with money now buy "moto-boats," motorboats, but most people just go out on the canoes or wade with their nets in the ocean or the lagoon. At times, the ocean can look aquamarine, almost teal, and you see men standing out not too far from the shore checking their fifty-foot-long nets to see what they've caught since they put them out.

Women will repair these nets, but they'll also make beautifully crocheted slips with lace made out of this same fishing line material. I receive no less than five of these slips, some with my name crocheted into the lace. More often, I see women sitting on their *buias* working thousands of strips of pandanus into gorgeous designs for mats. They know the geometric shapes that certain weavings and foldings of the pandanus strips will make even when they have no drawing beforehand.

Occasionally a small sketch will be made if someone wants to know what the finished mat will look like. The darker colors on the designs are made by boiling the pandanus leaves with old tin cans in big cast iron pots to dye them. My friend Emeri will sit on the ground or in her *buia*, weaving mats for her older daughter, Kamoia, who is away at secondary school on Abaiang island. Emeri sits, feet splayed, mat on her lap, manipulating hundreds of strands she is working on, which have gathered between her outstretched legs.

Sometimes when I go to the Bainuna village *maneaba*, the women will be waiting for a nutrition education session, or they'll just be sitting in the *maneaba* when there's no village, church, or other meeting or *botaki* going on. Here, they have the space to spread out their weaving, or other projects, which are usually for their own family's use, not generally for commerce. For the simple new *inai* mats, which are used on the floors of their homes or to hang as blinds, they gather palm fronds and quickly go to work. The *inai* require a young, almost light yellow green, coconut palm branch that's been hacked down from the tree. The leaves themselves feel like silk. I watch the women sit with legs spread out, long fronds spread out in front of them, hands gently plaiting the leaves.

The *inai* are always soft on your feet, and after a few days they turn from green to brown; then, after a while, they turn dark brown and sometimes get kind of damp, as does everything here on the equator. Then it's time to make more *inai* and throw away the old ones. Throwing them away means they either get burned with the rubbish, get used in the compost for *bwabwai* pits, or go into a pile of natural rubbish, leaves, coconuts, and seaweed that accumulates near the beach and eventually becomes compost itself or gets washed out to sea. Both men and women work in the bwabwai pits, but only men harvest this giant swamp taro.

The men also make eel houses, traps that look like small houses with an entry hole. They leave these out on the reef where the eels congregate. When the eels swim in, they can't get back out, and then the men collect the eel houses and there's more eel to eat. Men will also make fish traps. There are natural and handmade fish traps that are oftentimes huge stones arranged in a circle in the lagoon with one narrow opening. The fish swim in and then can't figure out a way out. You go inside and catch a fish with your bare hands, whack it over the head on a stone, and voila, dinner. I do this once at the trap in the lagoon area between Norauea and Bainuna villages.

The men also work at the backbreaking labor of cutting copra, the dried meat or flesh of the coconuts. The *Kiribati Environmental Science Pupil Book* explains it best. "Copra comes from a mature nut. It becomes copra when the kernel dries. The kernel is the flesh of a coconut. There are two ways by which copra can be produced. One way is to break the shell of a mature nut, leaving the kernel in its shape, which is called ball copra. The other way is to split the coconut in halves and when the kernel is dry, it is called cup copra, because it looks like a cup."

Coconut trees grow in Kiribati the way cacti do in the desert. The men head out to the bush to chop down coconuts carrying machetes and burlap sacks. Sometimes they go out on their bicycles and come back balancing the sacks of coconuts on the bars of their bike. Other times, a family or a section of the village will pool money and rent one of the island's two flatbed trucks to haul lots of coconuts home. The men come back and hack open the nuts. Thousands and thousands of coconut chunks are left lying open in the sun on mats or tarps on the ground. After a few days they're no longer white, but rather a dirty gray color, all dried up. They're left out in the sun and brought in if it looks like it might rain. The women sometimes help take care of the copra shards once they're lying in the sun, moving them to areas where they'll get maximum sun, or covering them if it looks like rain will come.

When the cargo boats come, on an irregular basis I haven't figured out, villagers haul burlap sacks of these chopped up coconuts to the docks to get weighed. Then they're paid pennies for all this backbreaking work. These small ships collect this copra from all the outer islands and bring it to Tarawa, where it's taken to Europe and overseas, making copra the largest export of Kiribati in 1999. It's used to make coconut oil, which is used in cooking oil, soap, benzene, perfume, and shampoo. Copra cake is also used as food for animals.

The only men who don't do much of this work are those from other islands, or who don't have *bwabwai* pits or coconut trees on family land somewhere on Marakei. The nurses and government workers and some of the teachers make enough income to not have to cut copra. Those in these professions, originally from Marakei, will do some of this on their own family land, but are not obligated to, as they have enough income from their jobs to get by without doing this work. My friend and colleague, Mareko, a head nurse on Marakei, does not cut copra, harvest his own *bwabwai* nor go fishing. He and Emeri are gifted these things by extended family that live on Marakei, such as Tuutana's family. They also get many things from people who come to the clinic and are grateful to Mareko for the free medical care he gives.

CHAPTER EIGHT

Problems addressed in my work tend to be lack of proper nutrition, lack of hygienic conditions, and lots of simple wounds that get infected. Or boils. The villagers pop them, and dirt gets into them. Oftentimes, simple wounds and boils turn into bigger deals because of these infections. Much of the health education efforts need to be targeted towards young women and mothers. They are generally the primary caregivers. (They call the women with young children *te tia tobwa*, the breastfeeders.) Kids also often have conjunctivitis on what seems to be a regular basis, though I never know if it's because conjunctivitis is so contagious, or because there's so much dust and dirt that gets kicked up in the air and can get into their eyes. Also, sometimes they'll touch or rub their eyes with fingers that haven't been washed.

I do simple public health educational sessions, or speak to people individually, encouraging villagers to boil their water to prevent water-borne illnesses. There are also food-related illnesses, such as diabetes, high blood pressure, and obesity.

Mareko and I urge them to eat more vegetables and a more varied diet, in general. Also, there is a need to eat more food with vitamin A, as many villagers have a deficiency in vitamin A, and get night-blindness and a reddish tint to their hair. I work with villagers to make green vegetable gardens, and we get seeds and cuttings donated from FSP, the Foundation for the South Pacific's Tarawa office.

Teaching about health during pregnancy, Mareko and I create a play about a Miss X, a young pregnant woman who dies of placenta previa, from lack of good prenatal care. The villagers like seeing other villagers they know acting in the play.

I try to do some teaching with the wives of seamen about AIDS. The young men who get jobs overseas on German and Japanese merchant marine vessels, go away as seamen for a year or two at a time, stop in many ports, and bring home gifts, which sometimes include venereal diseases and AIDS. Even though the ministry of health knows this, they can't figure out how best to address it. It is hard to even get people to acknowledge that AIDS is a problem to think about. There are maybe ten *known* cases of people who died of AIDS in Kiribati during 1998 and 1999. The men who work as seamen also leave behind wives who miss their spouses, and children who miss their fathers. Nevertheless, it is a good livelihood that they try to send home to their families.

Nei Teima, the island clerk, (which is equivalent to being the mayor, only she was appointed by the government and not the people of Marakei,) tells me a story about her son. Her husband is a seaman, working for the Japanese fishing boats, and away for months to years at a time. Ten Natan, her two-year-old son, always says to her at bedtime, "Mommy, *karaki*" (Mommy, tell a story), and she asks him what story he wants to hear. He always says *"Bapa"* (Papa or Daddy), and she tells him what it will be like when they meet Papa at the airport in Tarawa. How, when he comes back from overseas, they will go the airport and the big plane will land, and a man with sunglasses and long hair will get off the plane, and they will see him and it's Bapa/Daddy. Her kids don't know him because he has been away for so long. Teima says it puts her son to sleep every night to hear how *Bapa* will come to the airport to meet them someday. I hear this is a very hard way for families to live and my heart feels for little Natan and his siblings.

Not many people speak English to me outside of Rawannawi village, which houses the government employees, such as Teima, and the policemen. It is the largest of Marakei's villages. Tuutana and Mareko and other friends who understand English try to get me to converse only in Kiribati as well. Because of the cultural value placed on not shaming or embarrassing anyone, if someone speaks to me in English and their neighbor is sitting next to them and that neighbor doesn't understand, then the speaker is considered to be rude to their neighbor. Consequently, my use of English is limited.

Te katei (Kiribati custom) insists that visitors and foreigners should be made to feel welcome and valuable, so I sometimes feel villagers tell me what they think I want to hear when I ask them questions. I try to listen well, and I still wonder how this is going to fit in with my (and the Peace Corps) goals of not stepping on anyone's toes, and training and assisting locals to improve health education and promotion in rural areas. The government in Tarawa asked for a group of health education volunteers from Peace Corps, but the average villager on Marakei island has had little say in the matter besides voting for government officials and building the new volunteers their homes.

Someone usually helps me translate when I get to the health sessions, and village nurses and I make large health session posters with permanent markers on the backs of nylon rice bags. They say things like how to treat minor wounds, or how to make homemade oral rehydration salts if your child has diarrhea. Mareko, I, and village nurses organize health promotion skits, such as "Nei (Miss) X" and others, that travel from village to village. Also, the *Kamwengaraoi* (village welfare groups) and I start building community gardens.

Sometimes, Tuutana answers my questions and helps me figure out how to rephrase things in correct Kiribati. My neighbor, Teria, asks, "Why does my baby keep getting *te mata* (the worms)?" She tells me when we speak about it, "I want clean water, but I know from what you tell me that the water is contaminated because the distance between the wells and latrines is too short, my drinking water isn't always boiled, and the pigs and chickens poop near the water supply." I see that her life is busy, and she doesn't always have time to boil the water, and yet her baby is getting sick.

CHAPTER NINE

The slower pace of life on Marakei is good for me. I have some stability and peace, and even though I'm an outsider, I'm not experiencing the lack of meaning and hence, the "lost-ness" quality that had haunted me back in Florida.

I am busy with this new adventure, and spending quality time with people and outdoors. And I'm enjoying things going at a slower pace in Kiribati than in the United States. Additionally, my world, an island of 2500 people, is so much smaller than it would be in most cities in the U.S. I am happier and calmer here than I have been in a number of years.

The one thing that makes me anxious about Marakei, outside of just trying to do well at my job, is Anote. The newly elected member of parliament (M.P.) for Marakei, Anote, is Tuutana's relative. He is the brother of Martin, her grandmother Karorina's husband (the ones who live in Auckland). Anote was a convicted rapist in Hawaii, and spent two years in prison there. He comes back to Kiribati bragging about how he raped a white woman. He narrowly wins the Marakei election. Most people voting for him admit they don't like him but think he will bring in money for Marakei from the government in Tarawa, since he himself is very wealthy and has connections with a Korean merchant marine company. Anote's more charismatic than his opponent, Tuutana's father Anterea, and he gives people money every time he goes to visit them in their villages or homes, promising there will be more money if they vote for him.

Anote scares me. He comes to my house late at night and after a few instances of him banging on my door and harassing me, Tuutana's family starts hiding me when he comes out to the island. When he comes to Marakei from Tarawa, I spend whole weekends trying to avoid him, planning where I'll go and what I'll do in areas he'd not be likely to visit. Eritabeta helps me plan it all, and gets her daughter, Karetita, to tell the policeman to feed my pig, and to check the mail coming in on Friday's late afternoon plane to see if I have any packages.

Despite all this, Anote barges into my home one night with one of his supporters. He's upset about something I am working on with the *Kamwengaraoi* for health promotion. It is a project to get funding for *maneaba* wells and latrines, so villagers can have water and toilets when large congregations of people are staying in the *maneaba* for hours and sometimes days at a time (for large botakis, long meetings, church gatherings, etc.). Though approval was gained by consensus in the village welfare group meetings, Anote is upset he hasn't been consulted or asked for money. He doesn't want the government to help with something he can fund himself. He seems drunk, and his friend Betero takes him out when he starts lunging at me.

When I talk about this with the *Kamwengaraoi* groups, they tell me to "ignore Anote, and keep going on with what we talked about previously." Tuutana and her family also tell me to ignore it. She privately tells me to "steer clear of that bad man." No one wants to make a fuss. He's a crazy relative, and better not to speak badly about him. This I understand.

When everything comes up with Anote, people on Marakei start asking me regularly, "*Ko aki marawa?*" (Aren't you lonely?) They mean because I live alone. I want to say, "Yes, sometimes," but I really see it more as being a foreigner and a bit of that feeling of having one foot in one culture and one in another, not being native to their country or land, and I can't convey that to them without making them want to try to help me out...and it's simply the truth and not necessarily "fixable." Tuutana and her family ask me if I want to "sleep over" some nights in their large family sleeping structure: a large *maneaba* where all the kids and adults hang various-sized mosquito nets for everyone to sleep in within a 20-by-20-foot area. I stay over a couple times a month. We stay up late playing *te barawa*, dominoes, and then all fall asleep under different nets.

We'll be stringing up mosquito nets when the men come home late from fishing, the bottoms of their boats sometimes filled with flying fish. We see them hauling pushcarts piled with large flying fish, long tunas, or a big shark. Fish smell permeates the air. Sometimes Eritabeta throws flying fish on the fire, and we have a big feast at about one in the morning. The fish are black on the outside and tender inside and every other bite has you separating the tiny bones from the meat. Delicious.

In the morning, Karetita, Anterea and Eritabeta's oldest child, sits with other village women and teenage girls on the side of the road with old weighing scales, selling their husbands', fathers', brothers' fresh catch to those who haven't gone out fishing for the day's food. Nei Terenga's husband always brings in the most, since he has a motor for a "moto-boat." Flying fish, yellowfin tuna, mordekoi, and sometimes shark all go for five to twenty-five cents a kilo. People call out to me to come take fish when I run through the village in the mornings. I run back to my house dripping with sweat, flying fish in hand.

CHAPTER TEN

After a few months, Bauro leaves to go back on his ship. Tuutana goes to the airstrip to see him off but won't say much about it. She's still reticent to call him her boyfriend. She makes it seem like it's not a big deal, but she does write him letters. I am going overseas for annual leave at the end of August for a few weeks. Villagers joke with me before I leave to go on a visit to the States that, "maybe you'll take me with you in your suitcase!" Though I laugh, I know there's a slightly serious side to what they're saying, as many of them assume life is easier in America and everyone is rich, despite my protesting that there are poor people in America as well as elsewhere. Tuutana wants me to take more pictures of my family and where I live in America so she and her family can see what my life looks like there. I doubt pictures could ever convey all the differences.

I'm looking forward to going back to Minnesota and regrouping before I head into my second year on Marakei. It will be nice to wear Western clothes, to dance, to eat whatever I want, to have a glass of wine, to kick back, in American culture for a few weeks.

Before I leave for my trip, Tuutana starts asking questions about life in other countries. Karorina and Martin have sent her a videotape of a birthday party at their house in Auckland. When Anterea gets benzene, he powers up the generator, and Tuutana sits riveted to the television as the people in the video go about the business of cutting a cake, playing in the front yard, cooking in the kitchen, and eating at the kitchen table. She sees what their house looks like and what their neighborhood in Auckland looks like. To me, it looks like a nice, small tract home, with a well-kept lawn and long cement driveway, where they've parked one car. The neighborhood is full of homes this same size, from what I see on the video. It appears people take pride in their lawns and maintain their properties.

The conversations Tuutana has had with Karorina seem to have tripped a switch in her thinking. She asks me, "Does your family in America live in a house like the one in the video?" And, "Do they have a kitchen with a stove and a gas range like Karorina? And a yard with grass on it instead of coral rocks?" (instead of the coral rock ground covering here on Marakei, I presume.)

"Yes," I tell her, and I also say, "I'll take a picture of my parents' home for you to see."

While I'm at home in the States, my family throws my father a fiftieth birthday party. It's a huge party, and you could feed all of Rawannawi village on Marakei island for a year on the catered food alone. Grocery stores overwhelm me with their abundance of choices and fresh food, and I spend time trying to understand what friends are talking about with their "terminal-sitter" jobs working for dot-coms. In addition to getting treated for worms, I spend time shopping for all the items people on Marakei and Tarawa islands requested I try to get for them.

Reading the newspaper, I cut out something about Palm Pilots to show friends on the island and fellow volunteers. The need to be in constant communication via email, or beaming messages to each other, seems odd to me. Many things seem so impersonal, such as using an ATM instead of a bank teller, or having a job in a cubicle, where you mostly interact with computers instead of people. Back in Kiribati weeks later, fellow volunteers and I will chuckle about people being so frenetic about time that they need portable devices to "beam" messages to each other. We've obviously adjusted to the slower pace of Kiribati-time, as we think nothing now of waiting all day for the prop planes to show up somewhere between five and seven hours late.

In Minnesota, people get wide-eyed when I say I've seen a traditional bone healer on Marakei for my knee, which was strained from my daily runs through the village. They think what I'm doing is neat, but a little too remote for them to want to try.

I return to Tarawa and have a run-in with Anote, the MP, at a store, where he rants about getting me off "his island." He's about to fly out to Marakei, which makes me delay my own return to Marakei for a few days. I don't want to deal with him if I can help it. Anote has been harassing one of the other female volunteers, Yeekyong, and a few months later, she'll decide to terminate her Peace Corps service a full year early.

I've been told that Anote announced in some meeting on Marakei that he wants to kick me off the island because of the latrine project and his disapproval of it. Everyone says he's dangerous, but they get quiet when he throws money around, since who are they to bad mouth the person giving them money? Nothing comes from his making a scene, except that I get a nervous stomachache on one of the least violent and most hospitable of the Kiribati islands, whenever Anote comes to Marakei, which is usually once a month for a few days.

The Peace Corps directors on Tarawa issue a communiqué to the Marakei island clerk, Nei Teima, that Anote is not to have any contact with the volunteers on Marakei. I don't know what happened to that memo though, since it's never enforced and hardly seems enforceable. The realities are: villagers have little, money buys silence, and it's hard to miss white faces like mine in a sea of brown. Additionally, staying quiet about things is more important to the culture than shaming someone else, even if you don't approve of the other person's actions. This applies moreso if the person is someone like Anote, who could make their lives miserable if he chose to. The Peace Corps medical officer, who is a registered nurse, tells me, "If you're too scared, you can always terminate your volunteer stint, and return to the States." "No way," I say. "I'm not quitting! I'm fine." And the reality is, I am doing fine on Marakei, even with Anote.

My return to Marakei (from Tarawa, post my visit to the States) is weighted down, quite literally, with heaps of *bubuti'd* items. A *bubuti* is a request for help or items, that one makes to someone else or to some other group. If you say no to a *bubuti*, you embarrass or shame yourself in the process. *Bubutis* are often made in public places like the *maneaba* so there's public accountability. It's also okay to *bubuti* back for something from those you were *bubuti'd* by in the first place, so I back-*bubuti* upon my return and wind up with buckets of fresh lobster.

As part of a family, village, community, there's an obligation to bring the things people *bubuti*, if possible. I bring cake decorating kits, preschool toys, rosaries, saint medallions, and two sets of handcuffs for the policeman to use on arrestees. I have spent a goodly amount of time and money purchasing all the *bubuti'd* items in the States, not to mention getting severely overwhelmed at the Mall of America in a suburb not far from my parents' home in Minneapolis.

CHAPTER ELEVEN

Though I want Mareko to be pleased with the work I do, I see he doesn't work well with women, though all of his subordinates are female. He bosses Erea and Ruitia, two of the village nurses at his clinic, who happen to be sisters. "Nako, nako, go, go away," he yells if they make a small mistake, or don't know how to be of assistance to him in all instances. Sometimes I know that they often have to "look after me" when it comes to work, and yet I they know that I can help them occasionally with obtaining things that are harder for most Kiribati locals to obtain (when I go overseas or when I receive packages from overseas). When I first arrived on Marakei, their family also helped me to obtain fish, and to meet people. Mareko is very busy with his work though, so I have to ask him multiple times, though Emeri assures me "he is *mamamaninga*, very forgetful" so "ask him again and again."

When I go to a village and do a participatory health session with Mareko, trying to get villagers involved in their own education about some health topic, such as nutrition, he tries to redirect it to a strict lecture with him giving over the knowledge, rather than having villagers' input. This happens even when we plan a participatory session ahead of time, yet I know from what he's told me, that his schooling was done more didactically, in this way.

Doing health education sessions with him sometimes on topics, such as exercise, and watching one's sugar and salt consumption to prevent diabetes and hypertension, are a little counter-intuitive, as Mareko himself is overweight. He is extremely busy as the main nurse for the whole island, with assistant nurses stationed in farther away villages, and he does no exercise, and his job is fairly sedentary. In the same way we see sometimes in the States that doctors tell us to do something they don't always do, he eats a lot of food he would tell his patients not to consume.

Because of his position of power as the medical assistant on Marakei, people know they have to be extra nice to him if they want good medical care down the road, though it isn't supposed to work that way. He rides his new-ish *repe repe* everywhere, even to church, though he lives just down the road a little way from the Catholic church. He is nice to me mostly, though our relationship is a little stilted.

The reality of the new health education program, started with my group of Peace Corps volunteers by the Ministry of Education and Social Development, is that people here on Marakei are not certain if they should have me work only with the public health nurses, village nurses, island council workers, or village welfare groups. Or do I alternate between all of them? No decision is ever made, and I try to figure out a way to make my job work on Marakei.

It is hard to find a place or a main counterpart to work with, but I'm lucky to get to meet different and interesting villagers from various backgrounds this way, rather than being pegged to one organization or school. When I bike to the airstrip to meet the weekly plane and see if the mail bag was loaded on in Tarawa, I see people I know from each of the eight Marakei villages!

Tuutana bikes to my house, bringing fresh fish or lobster and we sit on the *buia*. She puts up the *inai* mats that shield the sun, but also keep people from being able to see everything you're doing. We eat these delicacies with fresh *bwabwai* and crummy packaged food like potato chips, SweeTarts, and frosting that I brought back with me on my trip. She jokes about having to eat it fast before all her sisters and brothers tromp over to join us. I tease, "*Ko kanna te I-Matang* food" (You're eating food from overseas). "And it's not even healthy food!" She laughs and says, "Yeah, but I like it with the taro and fish." So do I.

Still pining for junk food, I write to the Tootsie Roll company at the address on one of the wrappers that shows up in a parcel package sent from the States. I explain that I'm a Peace Corps volunteer who eats a lot of fresh fish and white rice and misses their product. I make sure to sell my plight and fit it onto a small blue aerogramme about how I would be willing to share Tootsie Rolls with all the villagers if their company would be kind enough to send some my way.

I apparently have too much hammock-time if I can make the effort to write letters like this, but three months later, Tootsie Roll Industries sends me a package with two hundred chocolate candies. Enclosed is a note saying they're always glad to hear from young American men and women serving overseas who say the taste of their candy reminds them of home. Now, I'm like the Tootsie Roll queen, always with a couple extra tied up in the corner of my *lava lava* or in my daypack in case I want a chocolate fix while hanging my handwashing out to dry or biking to a faraway village. I share them with my neighbors' kids and other villagers as well. I also write to the Kraft Company, and wind up with packages of instant macaroni and cheese.

As for news from overseas, I get the *Christian Science Monitor* sent to me for free, as part of a program they have for Peace Corps volunteers. Peace Corps mails all volunteers the international edition of *Newsweek* for the region where they are working, and Mom sends me old copies of the *New Yorker*. Radio Kiribati also has Australian Broadcasting Company headlines at the top of every hour, read in English. In the two years I am gone from the States, it appears much of the news there is focused on the Monica Lewinsky debacle, Kosovo, and the latest *Star Wars* movie.

CHAPTER TWELVE

Tuutana is curious in a different way now about the I-Matang. She is no longer at all shy around me. She tells me, "*Ko kaokoro. Ko kinna te katei ikai. Ko kanna te ben, te ika, te bwabai. Ngke, titabo te I-Kiribati*" (You, you're different, you learn the culture here, you eat the coconut, fish, and taro. You, you're like a Kiribati person). I'm honored, and notice she seems much less apprehensive than when we first met.

She tells me, "I can't imagine what my whole life will be like." I point out to her that, "If you stay here, your life will probably look a lot like Eritabeta's life. If you go to New Zealand, there are other opportunities that might open up for you." She just raises her eyebrows and says, "Eng, Amy. Yes, Amy."

Eritabeta is my rock here, though I see the tiredness in her eyes, and the weight she has never been able to lose from the six kids she has already given birth to by age twenty-nine. She has a beautiful smile and long, thick black hair, but she has dangerously high blood pressure, and does not listen to Mareko when he tells her that having more children may be a serious risk to her health.

Though not yet thirty, Nei Eritabeta looks like she could be around forty by American standards. The constant cycle of washing, cleaning, cooking, breastfeeding, and sometimes work outside the home in the council office or schools demands so much. I remind myself this is what many people here on Marakei see from the time they are little so this is their cultural norm. Tuutana tells me she can't imagine doing this for the rest of her life. Eritabeta calls her "tomboy," using the English word, all the time. She thinks of Tuutana as sometimes acting like a boy, because of Tuutana's independent streak.

I hear Eritabeta call Tuutana "tomboy" every time Tuutana runs off to play soccer or says she can't take care of her siblings. Eritabeta and her husband, Anterea, are proud that Tuutana did so well in school, and they're excited she may get a chance to go to New Zealand. The rest of the extended family also joke that Tuutana is tomboy-ish, to connote that she's a little wild and doesn't seem to fit into the "come-home-from-school-and-find-a-nice-village-boy" model of most girls her age.

Tuutana says, "I'm not ready to *iein,* to be tied to someone else," meaning, through marriage. She's still having fun, and she spends enough time with male cousins to meet their friends. Eritabeta loves Tuutana but realizes that Tuutana has had other parental figures in her life other than her and Anterea. There is Karorina in Auckland, and also Tuutana's biological father, Uni. She encourages Tuutana to write to Karorina in New Zealand and to spend time with Tuutana's own biological sister, Tobia, who lives with her own adoptive grandmother elsewhere in Rawannawi village.

Most days, Tuutana washes, cooks, cleans, looks after her siblings, plays soccer, and goes around with me to different villages for my work. She is done with school, unless she decides to go on to be a teacher or a nurse at some point. Then she would study at the Tarawa Teacher's College, or the Tarawa hospital's nursing training program.

CHAPTER THIRTEEN

Playing hygiene bingo with the women in the Bainuna village *maneaba*, Tuutana laughs at me. She thinks hygiene bingo is stupid, but these women are *seriously* into bingo. Who cares if each square says something like "*kaburo ran*" (boil your water), or "*tai beke iaon te bike*" (don't go to the bathroom on the beach), or "*kaitiakia baem imwin te beke ao imwain te amarake*" (wash hands after going to the bathroom and before eating)? They're all over it for the five cents Australian money the health clinic gives away as prizes. I'm pleased they'll listen to health messages without having to listen to my broken Kiribati.

Every week I'm asked in the *maneaba* or in passing, "Do you know Rambo?" with sincerity from various villagers. They always think I might be related to or know him personally. They think America is like Kiribati, where everyone knows everyone or is related to everyone and there's a total population of eighty-thousand something. When I tell them, "I don't know Rambo, and I don't know Sylvester Stallone," they look at me and ask, "He's not from your village?"

Villagers also find it interesting and are surprised when I say my family doesn't own guns. "*Kain America, a buaka aki akaka*," says T'Anterea, one of my neighbors. I think his and the general Kiribati perception is that, "those people from America make war, no matter what," is actually a fairly accurate description of what they hear about America from the radio waves and the videos they get.

I have to explain to T'Anterea, Eritabeta, and the rest of Tuutana's family one day, while we're watching videos, that Elvis is dead, and Ann Margret doesn't look like *that* anymore. They are all excited about the *new* video with Elvis in it they had received from someone overseas. They ask me, "Have you seen it?" which prompts conversation and curiosity over, "When did Elvis die? How old is Ann Margret now?"

Really, Amy, I think, you should have just kept it to yourself. After all, it *is* a new video to them.

One night, I'm sitting in the longhouse, watching a pirated version of *Titanic*, and the villagers all laugh when the crash happens with the iceberg. You can tell it's pirated, because you can see the heads of the people in the theater at the bottom of the screen, and when people in the theater get up to go to the bathroom as well. I whisper to Tuutana it's not meant to be funny; it's meant to signal that they're going to die, but everyone in the *maneaba* finds it hysterical and they are just laughing and laughing.

Also comical is that the village welfare groups tell me they want to give me a big birthday *botaki* party and feast for my twenty-eighth birthday. It strikes me that this is going to resemble one of those huge first-birthday *botakis* they throw for kids when they turn one, except it'll be a few decades later for me. Slightly embarrassing and truly enjoyable all at once!

Emeri makes me a blue satin sparkly party dress with white rickrack trim. I'm such a sight that Tuutana laughs and tells me I look "sooo pretty," but I can tell from her voice she's just elated it's not her they put in the dress. I wear it with my Cutter's bug spray, flip-flops, and an elaborate flower garland that the women handmake for my head out of frangipani and other fragrant flowers. Tuutana helps me memorize the long formal speech I have to give in the *maneaba* at the *botaki*.

I look like I'm seven in the dress, but the party is really fun. Everyone plays party games like the Kiribati-language version of "who stole the cookie from the cookie jar" and there's lots of twisting, the Kiribati style of dancing to deafeningly-loud popular Kiribati, and occasionally imported, recorded music. My twenty-eighth birthday finds me twisting away in my blue dress with scores of elder village men and women to the Kiribati-language dubbed version of the Macarena.

CHAPTER FOURTEEN

Every three to four months, I must fly to Tarawa for a week-long Peace Corps conference that includes further training or some aspect of volunteer continuing education, like increasing villagers' own involvement in personal and village health care. Though it's good to use the cold showers, as opposed to bucket bathing, and to buy ice cream at one of the small markets, I'm relieved to see Marakei from the air when I fly back.

Tarawa is a congested narrow strip of an atoll, where people from all the different Kiribati islands come and often live in squatter-like settlements. In an overcrowded capital with a growing population problem, people can't live off the land the way they do on the outer islands such as Marakei. There are a myriad of social problems in Tarawa tied to people losing many of their traditional ways, as Western culture impinges upon them. Children don't learn how to fish, and people forget the foods, recipes, culture, dances, and songs of their own islands once they move to Tarawa, problems that are much less visible on the outer islands.

I look forward to seeing Tuutana and her family and other friends on Marakei after being away. The smells of rotting breadfruit and fresh *kai-buaka* (stick of war) flowers greet me as soon as the plane door opens. *Kai-buaka* looks like the brilliant oranges, reds, and yellows of marigolds, and reminds me of cooking spices and a greenhouse all at once. I smell the flowers, the salty ocean air, and fresh food much more on Marakei than I ever do on Tarawa.

Tuutana, her sister Karetita, their friends, everyone's younger siblings, and I grate coconut into old *lava lavas*, and then twist and squeeze the meat inside the fabric into bowls to get coconut milk. We boil the creamy milk to make oil for our hair, leaving it in while we swim in the ocean. Then we all go back to my house and shampoo outside next to the water pump and my *buia*. We pump buckets and buckets of water so we can get all the oil and shampoo out.

The pump is actually two pieces of hollow PVC pipe, one inside the other, buried a few inches beneath the ground and attached to the side of the well with a foot valve twenty feet away. Pumping triggers the foot valve on the well to send water streaming out into the buckets. I've noticed it's a much better way to build upper arm strength than exercising with those silly two-pound hand weights I used before I came to Kiribati. The younger kids all shampoo and jump around singing to Radio Kiribati while it plays old-timey American songs like, "Rock My Soul in the Bosom of Abraham" and "Daddy Teach Me How to Pray."

I get lice at least five times, probably from falling asleep for naps on one of my neighbor's *buias*, on or near someone's lice-infected clothes and pillows. It's endemic on

Marakei. Everyone seems to have lice. My neighbors, Teretia or Nei Teria, pick them out. The cure is to wash hair with warm water and lots of shampoo. Only once do I have that special anti-lice shampoo from the Peace Corps medical officer, and it stings my head, so I give up on it.

Soccer season in the capital is gearing up, and Tuutana goes to Tarawa in November as part of the Marakei girls' team. The best male and female teams from each island go to Tarawa each winter to play in a series of matches. It's a big time for all the unmarried and under-forty-something crowd to hang out and meet each other. Our mutual friends share that Tuutana is able to talk to Karorina and Martin in New Zealand three to four times on the real phones available in Tarawa. It's a much better connection than with the Marakei CB (the one that sounds like a ham radio). We also see each other once in Tarawa while I'm there for a short conference, and we spend time with some of her family there, eating fish and rice, hanging out, watching an old movie. She is starting to talk more about going to New Zealand, and tells me, "I don't want to go alone."

"Why not?" I ask.

"It's my first time. I can get lost somewhere, *ao I aki bati n taetae n I-Matang*" (and I'm not great at speaking English).

I tell her, "I think your English is pretty good."

Tuutana says to me, "*Iai ana plan Nei Karorina moa, ibukin au mwakuri I New Zealand, bwa iai teutana te maku irou ibukin te mananga*" (Karorina's plan is for me to get work in New Zealand, but there is a small amount of fear in me about the journey). She tells me, "I'm scared to be in a strange place."

On Tarawa, Tuutana lives with Anterea's eldest son, Taneti, and Taneti's wife, Tetiria. She plays soccer everyday, hangs out with family, and talks to Karorina. She also talks to Bauro on his ship in the Pacific whenever he gets a chance to call her.

CHAPTER FIFTEEN

Back on Marakei, I start going to nightly singing practice in the Catholic *maneaba*. We practice songs for the *mwaie*, traditional Kiribati dancing, to be performed on Christmas day. Everyone knows I'm Jewish, not Catholic, but they welcome me to participate, and I understand that the history and stories of the Kiribati people, their islands and villages, get told through song and dance. Practice means hours of elaborate songs, calls, drumbeats on a large, hollow wooden box-drum, and dancing. The music can be so intense you lose yourself in the rhythms.

When I performed a traditional *buki* dance with two other female volunteers during Peace Corps training, I wore a huge pandanus leaf skirt, and other traditional dance costume regalia on my hands and arms. This year, I sing rather than dance, and feel more connected to the entire *mwaie* as I watch the dancers take turns rehearsing their performances and coordinating their hand, arm, finger, hip, and head movements to the music.

With my big skirt last year, I waddled more than danced.

The female dancers who are good coordinate each sway of their hips with the drumbeats and singing. They're beautiful to watch, and sometimes when they get into it, they scream out or cry during their dance. It's said they get, "*te ang*," that the wind or the spirit of the dance is within them. Months later, Eritabeta's mother will get "*te ang*" during the Easter *mwaie*, falling over with the spirit of the dancing, but she'll suffer a stroke afterwards and never wake up again.

Yeekyong and Brigitte go to Tarawa and overseas for forty-one days and Christmas break. I stay and have a beautiful Kiribati Christmas and New Year's 1999. It is nice to not have to hear villagers comparing the three of us, or tell me every little thing the two of them are doing. I hadn't realized how much this had become a topic of conversation. The villagers celebrate Christmas by going to church and watching and/or participating in the *mwaie*. The holiday is completely devoid of commercialism.

During the Christmas season and school break, I hang out with Emeri and Mareko's older daughter, Rebite, and her friend Katiria. Tuutana is still in Tarawa. Rebite goes to secondary school on the neighboring island of Abaiang. Katiria is the daughter of the village nurse, Kabwebwe. We take bikes to the wharf area where the men haul boats in late at night. We buy extra basins of fish for the big *botakis* happening in the Catholic *maneaba* at Christmas time.

There's a cool breeze out on the rocky shore area where the boats get pulled in, and we listen to waves crash as we wait for more fish-filled boats to come out of the water. Fifteen fish, each the size of my forearm, flop around inside my bicycle basket on the ride home. At least half will be salted and dried to make *tari*, a type of homemade tuna jerky.

Marakei is predominantly Catholic, but there is also a

sizeable population of Kiribati Protestant Church members as well. Additionally, many missionaries from overseas have made their way to Kiribati over the years, so there are small pockets of Jehovah's Witnesses, Mormons, and Seventh Day Adventists.

Many of the Catholics on Marakei are followers of the Legion of Mary, devotees of Mary. They have many gatherings to pray to Jesus and to Mary, and they say certain prayers centered on the life of Mary with regularity.

Villagers ask me all the time, "*Tera am aro?*" (What is your religion?) And when I answer, "Te Udaia, Jewish," their next comment to me is almost always the question, "When are your missionaries going to come here?" I explain that Judaism doesn't proselytize, and they then usually ask me, "How is your religion going to survive?" which is a valid question, though it hasn't been a problem thus far in Jewish history.

I have several Jewish prayer books with me in my stick hut, and I informally open and read from them from time to time. I also try to make a habit of lighting two small, narrow candles on my concrete and sand floor (so I don't burn down the hut) every Friday night at sundown, to welcome the Shabbat, the Jewish Sabbath. When I am in Tarawa, I light candles for Shabbat, and one time for Hanukkah with a fellow Jewish volunteer, Lena.

Anote, the scary M.P. still rattles me, but I have taken to, on my morning runs, doing lovingkindness meditation for myself, Anote, and others who upset me or are difficult. Somehow people have less power over me if I can wish them the kind of peace and happiness I would wish for myself. I decide Anote will probably still scare me, but my attitude can shift a little on him. And so I spend my morning runs concentrating not on my feet or my breath anymore, but on the phrases that repeat through my brain:

"May Anote be happy. May Anote be peaceful. May Anote be free from pain and suffering. May Anote be free from anxiety and grief. May Anote have mental happiness. May Anote have physical happiness. May Anote have ease of well-being." Though it may not completely change my overall fears or thoughts about him, for the period of time while I run, I find peace, and my heart expands a bit.

CHAPTER SIXTEEN

I START BECOMING FRIENDLY with Tuutana's cousin, Tekieru, and it's starting to become romantic, but since people don't really date here on Marakei, a relationship with him reminds me more of what it meant when I was twelve and people would say they were "going with someone." He's tall, dark, handsome, and funny, and is also related to Mareko, the medical assistant. Tekieru has been raised, in the Kiribati custom of relatives adopting other relatives, by his sister Kabwebwe, though he is still close to his biological father and mother. Kabwebwe is one of Mareko's village nurses, which means she is a local woman with basic training in weighing babies, assisting in doling out medicines, and performing other tasks that might help Mareko in the island's clinic.

Tekieru biological father, Te Taniela, is a *"te tia tabunea,"* someone who's good at magic, specifically white magic. People do lots of magic on Marakei, to get people to fall in love with them or their children, or to make people healthy. If they're doing black magic, it's often to make others sick.

The only thing I've seen is white magic, with elaborate rituals where there is cutting of the inner part of baby coconuts and the use of repetitive phrases said in a specific order, at specific times at night or in the bush. I have seen it work for good.

People believe in magic, just like they believe there are ghosts at night, and I find myself just observing and not questioning it. The gossip is that Te Taniela, Tekieru's father, is doing white magic to get me to fall in love with his son. Maybe they are right, because I am becoming a bit fond of him for a while. I know that there are villagers who known to be good at this magic, and I myself have seen people come down with illnesses very quickly, attributed to black magic; or people fall in love with others they barely know, which is attributed to white magic. I know very little about it except what I see and hear around me.

There are traditional views on sexuality in Kiribati. People are not openly gay or lesbian, but men considered (by themselves or others to be effeminate) are referred to as *penei p'n'aine*, and women who are more masculine are referred to as *penei p'mwane*. *Aine* is woman and *mwane* is man, and the word *penei* means "like," as in "similar to." People refer to these people by these names, but there is no overtly hateful speech or violence towards these individuals outside of the names. The labeling, from my limited vantage point as a non-Kiribati person living there, seems to be more of a statement of fact that this is a characteristic of theirs.

When Tekieru first kisses me, we are sitting in my hammock, and he looks at me and says, *"Ngai, I kan iein ma ngkoe,"* though I know even as he asks me to run away with him and be his bride, that we are not going to do that nor get married. I know it because what would he do if he ever came to the States? Cut copra and go fishing for flying fish, or steer an outrigger canoe somewhere? And, the fact that we're different religions is an issue for me. He is Catholic, a member of the Legion of Mary. And he is going off to become a seaman. I would never see him when he went away on year-long expeditions on German or Japanese ships around the world. Our backgrounds are very different, which would pose a problem at some point. Even though I am living in his culture for two years, I am still American. He will always be Kiribati. My logical mind knows this is not going to work even if it's been nice to get to know him.

The relationship ends when he leaves to become a seaman, and I'm not too upset. This is my first and only romantic relationship on Marakei, and it mostly consists of hanging out, kissing twice, and talking. We are never otherwise intimate together, and it never even poses itself as a possibility, though if it had, that would be the way to "become *iein*, married" in most Kiribati villlagers' eyes. Going without a romantic relationship is not the end of the world to me, though I don't see myself as staying single once I return to the States.

I try to talk to Tekieru about these cultural differences, and how they could create problems for us down the road, but he doesn't really listen. He repeats to me, the line, "I like you, *I tangiriko* (I love you). I want to marry you." After this, I don't see him for a little while, and then when we do see each other, we have to be careful not to give other people the impression that something might be going on, since villagers have wide eyes and large mouths about what is going on with the Peace Corps volunteer. It could be easy to get myself a bad reputation on the island if people were to spread gossip and I wouldn't want that.

After a while, Tekieru and I simply ignore each other because we are at an impasse and there are too many things that are hard to bridge, and the feelings aren't always able to be translated into words. Emeri and Mareko and a few others seem to be who I always ask questions about cultural things in Kiribati. I want to know if I am being respectful of the *katei*, the culture, so I ask them and get answers. Otherwise, how am I supposed to know that some things are okay to talk about, and others are *tabuaki,* taboo? They answer me honestly and help me navigate a way forward while trying not to upset anyone else nor get myself into a situation that might be more challenging later.

My bigger concern with this, though, is not if Tekieru is mad at me and why, but if my adopted family and friends here on Marakei are, and for this I am grateful they are not. Many of them have come to be good friends, and some of them are my work colleagues. I journal about it a bit and try to wish him well in my mind and in how I view the whole experience, but it does seem more confusing than it needs to be to me, and that might be both the cross-cultural barriers and my own internal feelings.

Tekieru gets into the Marine Training Center and leaves for training. He does come back to Marakei a few times on break from his schooling, and we run into each other on the dirt road on our bicycles. It's awkward, but we say hello to each other, and that's it. Emeri, in a very sweet way, says to me, "*Nei Amy, tiraua ataei n'mwane,*" and I know her telling me that there are lots of young, unmarried men is the Kiribati equivalent of "there are plenty more fish in the sea where that one came from."

Nobody talks very much about their feelings here, or discusses interpersonal relationships. From what I can tell, it is not a language with many words for various feeling states, and I find I'm not sure how I would express this to villagers in their language.

I do talk about my feelings about living and working here with my fellow Peace Corps volunteer friends when we get together for conferences on Tarawa. Peace Corps Kiribati doesn't have any sort of mental health counselor, or equivalent, though one could talk to any of the staff of Peace Corps.

When the World Health Organization sends a team of their doctors to the outer islands, including Marakei, to do widespread health diagnosis, and to help the medical assistant with his cases, they ask individuals from all of the villages on Marakei about their health and any symptoms and/or complaints they might have. One of the most common reported symptoms that people complain about is the feeling of emptiness. Young and old, married and unmarried, the complaint of emptiness is heard by these WHO representatives. The complaint is heard from Peace Corps volunteers on other islands as well. There are few words in Kiribati to express the gamut of emotions that would cover anything from "depressed" to "anxious." There is a word for sadness, and one for lonely, and one for scared, and one for empty, but there are no gradations of these emotions in the vocabulary that I can tell, and there is no overall known psychological language for people to plug their feelings into; hence, the complaint of emptiness when it might be differently described if one could get people to elaborate more.

There is no way to treat this problem on Marakei, or any of the other outer islands. There are maybe two psychiatrists from China working at Nawerewere, the only hospital in the country, in Tarawa, and they're busy with severe mental illness cases. There is no pharmacopeia of psychiatric medications for villagers to take to bludgeon their emptiness away.

Trying to get people to understand me, trying to understand them, not knowing what, if anything, is expected from me in different situations, and knowing I am alone as a foreigner, add up to a vast number of emotions from me though. I have a whole range of words in English to explain my frustrations and my experience with my work and life in Rawannawi village, but no one locally could understand what exactly I'm trying to say with these words. With some things, like with Tekieru, or with certain aspects of work projects here, I chalk up much of the experience to simple differences in communication.

CHAPTER SEVENTEEN

Tuutana returns to Marakei from the Tarawa soccer matches in January 1999. Her soccer team has done well in the finals, and she says, "I'm not leaving for New Zealand anytime soon." We tool around on our bicycles again, occasionally with Tuutana's younger siblings as "passengers" on the bars of our bicycles. The kids travel around the island and villages admiring things from the metal bar "seats" of my green roadster or Tuutana's beat-up blue Schwinn. I'm at Anterea and Eritabeta's house daily, or one of their six kids is at mine. Anterea has six other children from two previous marriages as well, many of whom are grown with their own children. I have a lot of downtime with my job, and the slower pace of life on Marakei means lots of "free time."

I ask Tuutana, "Why not travel with me?" Then she could just stay with her family there when I return to Marakei. We start to talk about going to New Zealand together, and what she will do there. She gets another video from her family there in a parcel with the VHS tape. It's a home video of some party, but at least she can see more of what their house looks like, and what their neighborhood in Auckland looks like.

I go to Tarawa for a Peace Corps conference and start thinking more seriously about, and planning, a vacation trip to New Zealand myself. It's a place I do want to visit. Tuutana, too, keeps talking about going, but she's scared to travel by herself. "What if I get lost?" is her mantra. "New Zealand," she says, "is too different, "*kaokoro mai ikai*" (different from here.)" I think it would be nice to travel with my friend, Tuutana, and I again ask, "Why don't you travel with me to Auckland? You can then stay with your family when I return to Marakei."

Karorina and Martin have saved for Tuutana's ticket since she finished school, but they either want to come from Auckland to Marakei themselves to accompany her, or to have someone from her family in Marakei escort her there. The importance of this to her and in Kiribati culture is never explained to me, but I make a genuine offer and let Tuutana think about it. After mulling it over, she cautiously brings it up with Anterea and Eritabeta on Marakei and with Karorina and Martin in New Zealand.

She has lived with Anterea and Eritabeta since Karorina went to New Zealand. Girls usually defer to what their male parent or guardian wants for them in making decisions like this. Anterea thinks this is a good idea, "because Amy has traveled overseas before," because I am close to her, and because "I think of you as a daughter too," he says to me. Everyone agrees it's okay for us to travel together.

I'm grateful that I have developed friendships and have people who treat me like family on Marakei. Some of Tuutana's friends have also taken me into their lives, and tease me in a good-natured way the same way they do to their family and friends.

Tuutana and I bike with Katarina, a Kiribati girl her age, and some of our other friends to swim under the bridge in Tekarakan village. The bridge over the passageway from the ocean to the lagoon is the same road that connects the village of Tekarakan to the village of Buota. You can dive off the bridge into the lagoon, and then swim the passageway out beyond the reef to the ocean. We swim in our clothes, and people laugh at me that I won't jump. I go down the long way underneath the bridge and wade in. They yell at Tuutana to teach me how to jump until they realize I'm just chicken. Tuutana just laughs and says she'll help me, "learn to jump someday."

By the time Tuutana's discussions, letters, and trips to Tarawa to talk to her *babako* are over, a few months have elapsed. If Tuutana leaves Marakei for New Zealand, chances are it's for good since she will then live as a "child" in her *babako's* house, probably until marriage, and perhaps afterwards as well. Meanwhile, I have an idea based on something she'd said about going to school once she got to New Zealand, that her going would give her a chance to explore greater educational options than those available to her in Kiribati.

"I think I'd like to study to become a math teacher," Tuutana tells me. "I did very well in math at school." She knows she will be spending lots of time with Karorina's family, and hanging out with Karorina's children, two of whom have been born in New Zealand, and whom Tuutana has yet to meet.

When I fly back to Tarawa for a conference, I book my flight to Auckland for a little over a month away. She comes to the airstrip to see me off from Marakei to Tarawa, and we discuss our plan. We'll meet in Tarawa, get our tickets, get travel details settled, pick up my soon-to-be-visiting dad, fly back out to Marakei, have a few weeks or so to say goodbyes, fly back to Tarawa, and then onto Auckland.

Once she flies to Tarawa, we call Karorina and Martin in Auckland two or three times. She informs them she'd like to travel with me so she'll feel more comfortable and safe. She has asked their permission, and she also asks them to explain how it will all work out in terms of paying for her ticket and the details of when we'd like to come.

Karorina and Martin wire the money for her ticket, and Tuutana and I are booked on the same flight in Tarawa at the small travel agency there. Tuutana has to get her birth certificate, her passport, a police clearance letter, as well as fill out some papers from the New Zealand consulate. She stays at her brother Atanuea's house while I stay at the Tarawa dormitory for Peace Corps volunteers. We go to her old school to get copies of transcripts and papers signed.

Two days before my father arrives, and our flight back to Marakei, she drags me across the entire Catholic secondary school campus she attended so she can get her school records. Squatting in the dust under the overhang of one of the many buildings in the compound, I think about how people here are oftentimes hesitant to approach church or other authorities, out of fear of bothering someone they think may perhaps seem more important than themselves. I know Tuutana is devoutly Catholic, and I can't figure out what the fear is exactly, since she talked about liking the school when she went there. She says the priests "were strict," and that's as much information as I get. She tells me, "*I maama*, I'm shy."

Crouching just out of sight of the priest, she's trying to determine if she can "bother" him for her transcripts. She thinks it's a good idea to have the transcripts with her when she leaves Kiribati, but, "I don't want to catch him at a busy time." "What if he doesn't remember me?" Meanwhile, I'm like a pushy parent in the dusty background, agreeing with her that it would be good and practical to have the papers just in case she wants to apply to school someday down the road in New Zealand. I urge her to, "just go ask him for copies." She eventually asks and obtains them.

Tuutana is keenly aware that life in other countries can hold more material riches and higher standards of health and education than on Marakei. She's also aware of what she'll be giving up in terms of her culture, family, heritage, and being part of a strong community if she leaves Kiribati for New Zealand. She's met enough foreigners, talked to enough merchant marine seamen, seen enough videos, and heard enough Radio Kiribati broadcasts of headlines from Australian news to be able to tell me, "Anything people want in these rich countries, they can go buy at the store. Life on Marakei is hard; it takes a lot of work." I just listen to her on this, since she's the one who has to decide.

She's right about the work that goes into getting food, getting water, and doing daily chores in Kiribati, and she's also correct in knowing she would be giving up a wealth of nonmaterial riches to go overseas. "*Akea te katei, akea te aba, akea te'ika, akea te bwabwai ikeike*," she keeps saying, and I know she means more than just that New Zealand doesn't have Kiribati culture, Kiribati land, plentiful fish, or giant swamp taro.

While Tuutana is at the police station getting documents, I go to the New Zealand consulate in Tarawa. Tuutana has asked me, "Can you talk to them and see if they can give me any information on visas and schools?" I speak with the gentleman working behind the desk.

"I have an I-Kiribati friend here who will be going to New Zealand, and she wants to get residency status there.

What advice or information on schools and visas can you give me to share with her?"

He looks at me, and I can tell he sees naiveté written all over my face. He's an Anglo married to an I-Kiribati woman, a fact I know since it's not a large expatriate community on Tarawa, and because most foreigners in Kiribati know something about the other foreigners on the atoll, even if they've yet to meet them. He speaks to me in a knowing way, about the dangers of assuming one place has more to offer than the other, saying, "It's the difference between getting a so-so education in a warm culture such as Kiribati, versus getting an excellent education in a cold culture, such as New Zealand or Australia." I know he's not speaking about temperature, and the volumes he speaks about cultural dislocation register within me.

CHAPTER EIGHTEEN

My father comes to visit Kiribati from Minnesota via Los Angeles, Fiji, and Tarawa. Dad, Tuutana, and I fly from Tarawa to Marakei, video camera, hefty luggage, and all. Anterea, Eritabeta, Mareko, Emeri, coworkers, and friends all meet him. He spends a week on the island and another three days in Tarawa. He videotapes the dancing and goes out deep-sea fishing with the men. My mother is not up for the trip, thinking, rightly, that it would be too rustic here for her. She sends goodies, such as Cadbury Fruit and Nut bars and M & Ms, for me in Dad's luggage. Dad swims in the lagoon and gives a thank-you speech in English, which I translate, in the *maneaba*. He thanks people for being so nice and helpful to his daughter.

Villagers and friends say to me, "We're so glad to meet your father. We know if someone comes to check on his daughter, he is a good father and a good man." The fact that I haven't lived with my parents in years makes no difference to them. The male patriarch coming to visit and "checkup" makes much more sense to them, and in a sense is one way of legitimizing me and my role here. They can understand me as a single woman in Marakei once they see that my father cares enough to visit and meet the people "taking care of his daughter." Of course, this is both my perception, and some of what is relayed to me in the I-Kiribati language.

Dad's video camera is in near-constant use. He videotapes Tuutana saying, "I'm glad to know Nei Amy, and to meet her father," (in English, for his benefit.) Friends have a few big *botakis* welcoming him to the island. I've tried to keep it as low-key as possible, knowing he has severe arthritis and won't be able to sit for so long. I tell people he'll need a chair, with which they seem fine. I kind of wish I'd said that about myself, a simple, "I need a chair," a year before, but now I'm fine sitting cross-legged.

Dad seems to enjoy himself, but when they talk long in Kiribati *at* him, he doesn't wait for me to translate, but just walks off with his video camera, even if they're in mid-sentence. He sits on the *buia* and points the bottoms of his feet at people, which is a big cultural no-no, though how would he have known? I explain it to him after. At my house, when Tuutana, Katarina, and I make dinner for him one night, he won't touch the salad made from my own home-grown bok choy, as he's trying hard to stay healthy and not eat things he's unsure how his stomach will do. I do rinse my home-grown vegetables with boiled water, but he is only here for a short while and is extra cautious, mostly eating cooked fish and other items. In watching some of the way Dad takes in cultural things as a visiting tourist, I can see a bit of myself in the first few weeks of my time in Kiribati, almost a year and half earlier than this visit from my father. As a short-term traveler, one doesn't necessarily have to, nor want to, adapt to the way the local culture handles things or does things. It's a fascinating reflection point for me to think about given that I intentionally relocated here longer term, albeit only for a few years.

At this point in my service, I find I am getting more well-versed in Kiribati manners, as well as language. The former consists of things like never passing something over someone else's head, never pointing the bottoms of one's feet at someone else in a *maneaba* or on a *buia*. And always getting off your bicycle on the road, and walking the bicycle past any *maneaba* when people are gathered inside for a *botaki* or meeting.

Dad spends his time on Marakei sleeping in my stick hut and using the pit latrine, and managing not to get sick, a feat in and of itself. On the food issues, I have to hand it to him, because though he's not adventurous with his food, he drinks lots of *moi moto*, the young green coconuts good for oral rehydration, as an antidote to stomach troubles. Myself, I try everything people offer me and have intestinal problems.

Dad spends lots of time walking the island, video camera in hand, taping dancing and kids playing homemade games on the road, with things such as found tin cans and rope. He goes out in the ocean with Beatirike's husband, TeNikora, on a traditional canoe. They haul in a few tunas, he tells me, that are "the size and length of a large ten-year-old." But he's visibly shaken when they come back to land. He thinks he should have brought a life vest, especially when he hears about a *wa*, a canoe, that has gone out and never come back. I have a Peace Corps issued life vest, which has never been used in the two years I've been here except as a cushiony pillow in my hammock. "Amy, we were out really far, miles from anything," Dad says when I tell him, "people don't know from life vests here," but I'm sorry I hadn't thought to offer it to him. After that, we go on traditional canoes in the lagoon, where it's more like a big lake in the middle of Marakei and there are no waves.

Dad and I also almost drown in the ocean when we go out with the men free diving. Neither of us knows how far out they're going to go. And though we're just floating, snorkeling, and swimming on the surface, we drift out a little too far and have a hard time overcoming the current and getting back in. The men come in from free diving bringing back octopi and lobsters.

Villagers think my dad's a giant at six foot two. Until they tell me this, I haven't really thought about people's height here, but they're right. I notice that Dad is visibly taller than most Kiribati men and women.

Back in (the capital island of) Tarawa a few days later, I take him to see old rusting Sherman tanks and rusty twin engine planes from the World War II Battle of Tarawa sitting in the ocean. We take a small tour of the places where most of the U.S. Marines were killed, see some still-standing Japanese bunkers that people in Tarawa have built their homes around, and we also see current Marine and ANZAC memorials. We wade out at low tide and Dad finds a piece of a tank that has a bullet hole shot through it, and we find some small shell casings that have coral crusted on them. They've been sitting there since 1943. We donate the piece of the tank to the small museum and take pictures in front of the other tanks and rusting twin engines. While out in the ocean at low tide, I make a short video letter to my Bubbie, my grandmother, and family back home.

CHAPTER NINETEEN

After Dad leaves Kiribati, Tuutana and I fly to Tarawa where we get her final papers in order. I make copies of everything for her, help her find a good travel bag, and make sure people have our itinerary. She buys a pair of flip-flops for the plane, since I keep telling her they probably won't let her board the international flight in her usual bare feet (both on Marakei and Tarawa). We get two huge buckets of tuna and paddle fish and *bwabwai* for her relatives in New Zealand, which we pack in lots of ice and drop off the day before our flight at the fisheries inspection building at Kiribati's Bonriki International Airport in Tarawa. Tuutana *bubutis* her family on Marakei to send food for her final going away *botaki* in Tarawa the night before we leave, and they send in big rice bags with her name on them full of *bwabwai* and *mwanai* (land crabs) on the Marakei-Tarawa plane.

The big day arrives. Tuutana has on a new outfit made by her relatives. It has huge yellow and black flowers and squiggly lines going every which way on it. She wears it over her black spandex biking shorts and gray t-shirt. I wear a new floral blouse under my overalls. This is the second time I've worn pants since I got to Kiribati a year and a half ago. Between the two of us, we're wearing more garlands of flowers than I've seen frangipani trees on Tarawa. I have on what feels like a half kilo of cowrie shell necklaces hanging around my neck, gifted to me by Kiribati friends. Tuutana has some on as well. She tells me she's nervous and "*I kan i mumuta* – I could vomit."

At Bonriki Airport in, we wait for the Air Nauru flight to Fiji. Meanwhile, half the Peace Corps volunteers serving in Kiribati are also at the airport; we're all going to different points in the Pacific for vacation. I'm the only one traveling with an I-Kiribati person. Tuutana has one small carry-on bag with her stuff. Most of the things she wears, has, or uses are really her family's things--family either in Tarawa or out on Marakei island respectively. She tells me, "It's like they'll be my family now," referring to Karorina and Martin in New Zealand. She travels light, as she's seen a video of their Western-style home in Otahuhu, Auckland, and imagines they'll have everything she needs.

We check my large bags and make sure our buckets of fish are put in the queue of bags waiting for the Air Nauru flight. We see our food cargo, these two huge buckets of fish and *bwabwai*, sitting out in the sun. I joke with my Peace Corps friend Kayla, who has come to the airport as well. "I never thought I would be responsible for so much exporting of fish and taro in my life." We're weighed with all our bulk, standing on old rusting scales to see if we're over our limits, calculated by our own body weight plus carry-on baggage.

An announcement crackles over the loudspeaker in the open-air airport with its series of semi-enclosed low structures. The plane has been overbooked by Raoi travel, the only travel agency in all of Kiribati. Air Kiribati, which operates boarding procedures for the travel agency, starts calling names to stay. "Those people whose names are called will have to try to get a seat on the next week's plane, but there is no guarantee there will be a seat, only that we can get you a refund or that the tickets will eventually be honored," drones the voice on the loudspeaker. I feel the crowd getting tense and anxious. No one wants their name called. Planes don't make it out here regularly enough to want to chance waiting, plus the buildup of going overseas has the crowd excited. People start pushing up towards the one ticket counter.

"Takke Tebuaka. Meria Tebwe. Tuutana Uni," the names go on. Tuutana's name is called to stay. Foreigners apparently get preference because only I-Kiribati names are being called over the loudspeaker. I find an officer and explain in Kiribati, "I'm traveling with Tuutana Uni, so she can meet her *babako* in New Zealand. They're expecting us to come together." Surely, he will understand that for both cultural and personal reasons, her traveling with me is something she and her family on Marakei and in Auckland expect to happen. On today's flight, not on separate ones.

He looks at me and says, "No. You can choose to forfeit your ticket and try to get on next week with her, but there is no guarantee. She must stay."

I try to calmly explain, "They're waiting for us. They're expecting us to come together. Her family doesn't want her to travel alone. She doesn't want to travel alone. We can't wait until next week. She paid for her ticket, and we booked them together."

He says nothing but looks to try to assist the next person crowding up to his counter. "See here," I start gesturing.

"Seats 12A and 12B. Together. You know that *ana koraki*, her family, in Auckland will be *very* disappointed if she doesn't come today."

I know that after months of preparation and all of Tuutana's anxiety, she won't want to do this again. She'll just say, "*E aki mwakuri*, it didn't work out." And the ticket will sit and wait until someone else can go with her. Or, more likely, I fear, she won't go.

My tactics aren't working. Ten Kairibo, the boarding agent, isn't buying my argument. By this point, I've figured out that there are many seats that Raoi travel has double-booked and I point this out to him, asking, "Who bought their seat first?" He has no answer to this. I say, "I understand that nobody tried to have this happen and that there's been a mistake, but I don't see why Tuutana should have to give up her seat purchased far ahead of time because of an honest travel agency mistake."

He looks at me again and says, "No. She has to stay," with an air of bureaucratic arbitrariness about it, and you can tell he doesn't want to deal with me. My voice gets shrill, and I loudly say to him, "There's no point in me going without her if the whole point of her going now is to have someone she can travel with. Surely you can understand that. It's part of your *katei*, your culture," knowing he will at least agree I-Kiribati people prefer to have girls and women travel with others rather than by themselves.

Tuutana quietly says, "It's okay, Amy, I'll try to go next week," but she's actually sobbing, and when I ask her quietly what she wants, she tells me and then Kairibo, the agent, "Please. I want to go on this flight. With *her*." She points at me. Much later, she'll laugh when she tells the story, "Amy, *I maku, bwa ko un* – Amy, I was scared, but you were angry."

We move away from the counter and stand, with our

little posse of both I-Kiribati and some Peace Corps friends, near the open area where people wait to board. It looks like a big animal pen, and people are upset about the tickets, but in Kiribati style, most of them just say, "*E aki mwakuri. Ti na kataia riki n te wiki e na roko.* It didn't work. We'll try again in a week."

Tuutana is still carrying her one small backpack of personal belongings. She takes off the flip-flops we bought for her ahead of time. "They're uncomfortable," she tells me, dangling them in her hand. My luggage and our fish and *bwabwai* are still sitting out on the tarmac. I look at all the stuff out there and think about all our preparations and again ask her privately and quietly, "Do you want to go now if we can get it to work?"

"Yes," she says through her sniffles and sobs.

After a few more hours of waiting, they start calling for people to board the actual Air Nauru plane, but there are no row or seat numbers being called, and no one is even checking people's tickets. I look at the people walking towards the plane and see that neither the boarding agent nor the policemen are even paying attention to anything involving the passengers themselves. No one is even collecting tickets. Those people on the flight are just walking towards the plane, now that the simple metal gate is open. It feels scary to me, but I look at Tuutana, and I say to her, "Let's move," and she doesn't budge. I say quietly, but firmly, "Get on this plane with me because you have a connecting plane in Fiji to New Zealand, and don't worry about it." And she's crying. I think to myself that I might get in really big trouble with the police. All our friends are looking at us to see what we'll do.

"*Move,*" I say again. "Let's go." And Tuutana nods. She wipes the tears from her face, puts her shoes on, and we both walk out as calmly as we can towards the plane.

Climbing the stairs to the plane, she looks back and waves to her family and friends. Then she turns to me and asks, "Amy, what if we get in trouble?"

"I don't know, but I don't think we will," I tell her. She turns back and keeps going towards her future.

At the top of the steps to the Air Nauru plane, the steward tells us," Sit anywhere you want. There are plenty of seats." We find seats and the Nauruan steward is overly solicitous, asking, "Do you want anything drink? Do you need extra pillows?" He tells Tuutana, "Someone from Raoi will probably get in trouble for the problems with this flight." Tuutana looks like she's beside herself with anxiety, her eyes flitting around and she seems jumpy. She quietly says to him, "My name. They called my name. Is it okay I'm here?" I don't know if he understands her, but he looks at her ticket that she's holding out to him and says, "You're fine, Miss." And with that, she settles down.

We arrive in Fiji and find they've rescheduled our flight from Nadi, Fiji, to Auckland until the next morning, so we're put up at a hotel. Everything is new and somewhat scary to Tuutana. She seems to proceed with caution. The two large buckets of fish and taro, both of which are sealed in plastic bags, are not going to make it a night in our hotel room, especially after being in the sun and then the cargo hold. I ask the hotel staff, after being prompted by Tuutana, "Can we put the fish in the hotel's deep freeze and repack them in fresh ice in the morning?" I'm up for abandoning the fish, but Tuutana refuses, and I respect that. It's one of the few tangible things she's able to give to her family in Auckland, something that tastes and smells like home.

The hotel clerk looks at me like I'm nuts when I pull fish after fish from one bag and put them in another. Tuutana and I have dinner at an Indian restaurant at the hotel, and she's curious about the restaurant scene, taking in china plates and papadam, and the way people are dressed. She steadfastly refuses to use the escalator, not trusting moving stairs.

The next day, we land in Auckland and the woman at immigration puts on plastic gloves to stick her hands down fish mouths and inspect our stuff. Tuutana's amazed people need to check to make sure we haven't done something funny or smuggled anything in amongst the foodstuffs. She asks, "Why would people ruin good fresh fish by sticking something inside them?" Of course, we also had to bring someone's *kamaimai*, toddy boiled until it forms into a maple syrup-type mixture, which has opened up all over my clothes.

Tuutana's family and relatives meet us in Auckland. Tuutana and Karorina are both overwhelmed and start crying. Tuutana has never met any of Karorina and Martin's five children, all of whom have been born in New Zealand. We ride in their Chrysler from the airport, and they tell me they kept putting off Tuutana's arrival even though the money had been saved, because they knew she was scared to travel alone. Martin stares at Tuutana in the rearview mirror, seemingly amazed the stubborn little girl he knew when she was young has grown up. He hasn't seen her in over ten years. "Why did you give yourself that tattoo?" he asks about the small black dot beauty mark she tattooed right between her eyebrows when she was in high school.

It's approximately where a woman might put a bindi on herself, and Tuutana did it the same way everyone in Kiribati tattoos himself or herself: by taking old black rubber tires, boiling part or all of the tires until they get a black runny dye, and then taking a needle or knife and carving out the design or dot or initials they want on their skin.

Then they paint the rubber dye into the place they've cut, making sure to keep scraping away any scabs that form on the skin until the area scars up and forms a tattoo. I smile to myself, because I can tell that both Karorina and Martin care about what she does to herself.

Karorina and Martin live in a modest home in the Otahuhu section of Auckland, an area with a high percentage of Micronesian immigrants. Martin and the boys have landscaped the yard, and they have a family dog and three ducks. The children all go to Catholic schools. Karorina stays home with the younger children while Martin works for a large New Zealand metal company. Martin has two siblings who live within a few miles, with their spouses and children.

There is to be a big *botaki* with their Kiribati family and friends to welcome Tuutana in two days. Customs can travel to new countries, as I see their living room substitutes for a *maneaba*/longhouse. Store-bought lamb, meat, or the occasional slaughtered pig bought from a farm substitute for pigs raised on one's own land on Marakei. We still eat lots of fish in New Zealand, store-bought rather than freshly caught, but by now I'm used to eating raw fish, cooked fish, sautéed fish, grilled fish, or boiled fish for breakfast, lunch, and dinner.

Tuutana's a little homesick, but she tells me, "I don't want to talk about it." A few days after we arrive, we drive to the top of Mount Eden to see the city from a great vantage point. After going to the mall twice, I'm overwhelmed by the speed of Western culture. Tuutana keeps walking around like she's in a trance. One of her biological mother's relatives comes up from the city of Palmerston North, and we all go on a tour of major points on the North Island. So now, on top of Tuutana seeming to be reeling from the changes, she has a long-lost relative talking to her about her biological mother, who died when she was very young. She's hardly feeling excited about being here, though this starts to lift as we go and do more and she gets to meet more people.

Martin and Karorina are only in their mid-thirties, and act much more like Tuutana's parents than grandparents. Martin's been working for the same company for ten years. He has moved up the ranks and been able to find jobs for different family members in the company, as they have come over to New Zealand from Kiribati. The owner of the company seems to like Martin and has agreed to sponsor Tuutana's application for residency.

Without my bringing up the subject, both Martin and his two siblings in Auckland manage to tell me in a roundabout way to avoid their brother, Anote, on Marakei. Martin's sister, Thea, says to me, "There are sometimes people in power who we know can be dangerous to be around or alone with on Marakei." It's cryptically said, but a clear message, and it echoes Tuutana's telling me months earlier, "Steer clear of that bad man."

Karorina has decided not to learn how to drive, so I'm designated as our daily driver. Karorina, Tuutana, and I drop Martin off at work, the kids off at school, and head out for the day. Karorina's English is good, but she's hesitant to use it. Martin uses it all the time because he speaks it at work. The children are all bilingual in Kiribati and English, but only the older two boys still answer their parents' Kiribati questions with Kiribati answers. The other three children always answer Karorina in English. Tuutana tells me she thinks her English is worse than that of the five-year-old daughter Biritia.

I drive us to a museum where we have lunch in a

cafeteria. The cashier is rude, almost refusing to help Karorina, but is overtly nice to me a few moments later. Karorina gets flustered, saying it's because of her accent, but she glances at me when Tuutana's eyes are turned away. I understand, from her eyes and gestures to me, that what's just happened to Karorina might happen to Tuutana in various places in Auckland where people may discriminate because they resent immigrants and are unkind. Tuutana doesn't understand the cashier was possibly being racist, and Karorina doesn't want to try to explain it to her in her first week here.

I'd like to see more of this country outside of just Auckland, and Tuutana and I talk about taking a few short trips while I'm still here. The two of us take day trips to see sheep shearing, and we go to Rotorua and the Waitomo Glow Worm caves. Tuutana's interested in learning more about traditional Maori dancing, and how Maori women, like Kiribati women, also make dance costumes out of native plants that they roll, dye, and weave. She tells me, "I'm starting to feel a little less homesick." But she also says, "Maybe I'll try to go back to visit Marakei for Christmas 1999." That's seven months from now. I can relate to these mixed feelings, after having felt this way, off and on, during my time on Marakei.

Everywhere we go, Tuutana wants to get photographed, which happens a lot on Marakei too. People wait months until I get developed photos back from the States because they think it's great to have pictures of themselves. Tuutana hams it up for the camera, and we wind up with some funny pictures of us at different tourist spots. I realize both of us are shy at first, and once we warm to other people, we have moxie and a mischievous sense of humor.

Lying on bunk beds in the extra bedroom, we talk at

night about her staying in Auckland and me going back to Marakei, and she tells me she thinks of me as a sister. "*Titabo te rara*, Amy." (Same as blood, Amy.) I am reminded that we "choose" our family as we get older, and our friends can become our family, just as much as the family we are born into.

CHAPTER TWENTY

I RETURN TO KIRIBATI for the final nine months of my stint as a volunteer. On my return trip, after my time in New Zealand, I am again loaded down with gifts, this time from Tuutana to her family back on Tarawa and Marakei. I'm like a pack mule. My departure is full of emotions, since I'm excited for Tuutana, and I'm also sad to leave one of my best friends in Auckland, and uncertain how it will be to return to Marakei this time. I know I'll miss her when I'm back there.

Life on the Kiribati islands is often full of moves from one island to the other, often with limited communication between friends and family. It feels like a nomadic way of life because of the distance between atolls and the lack of easy means to communicate between them. I have seen many people come and go in the little time I've been here, and I know that, though I hope Tuutana and I will stay in touch, I've seen this transient nature of people's lives here in the islands and I'm aware of how staying in touch with each other can be challenging at best here due to limited communication and communication modalities available.

Once I'm back on Marakei, I wonder when Tuutana and I switched from being friends and her helpfulness towards me, to my being helpful to her. When we first started biking together, she was not only my escort, but she also explained things to me culturally here and there, easing my transition.

By the time my father came, we were very good friends, but she also helped me with taking him out to Marakei, and helped with cooking big Kiribati-style meals for he and I and friends, which I'd only been doing previously in small quantities. She helped me figure out whose *repe repe* to rent while Dad was out on Marakei, knowing we could never just borrow the island council one, and that my father, at age fifty, qualified as an *unimwane* (an old man) who would probably not want to bicycle around the island as I usually did.

When we arrived in Auckland, I was feeling like a combination of friend, advocate, pushy mother and person who wants the best for someone they care about, and wondered how all of that had happened. We returned to a more even keeled calm and connection as we traveled around New Zealand and Tuutana became a bit more acclimated. I hope that our relationship and friendship continues over time.

Things work out fine with my remaining time on Marakei, sans Tuutana. I help out a little at Nikierere Primary School, teaching environmental science, and doing my health education sessions. I am generally happier with two Peace Corps goals--learning about the host country culture, and teaching about American culture—than I am with the actual job, which is good, but sometimes vague. I start teaching the Virtues program, which is a New Zealand-based program that takes virtues like trustworthiness or faithfulness or friendliness, and translates them into Kiribati words that have equivalent meanings, in order to teach these virtues or values in the villages. It is seen as a way to teach ethical behavior to combat things like family violence and excessive drinking to oblivion, and possibly assist with coping skills. I don't know about the effectiveness, but the teachers at the schools and the catechists at the churches all want me to teach it with them, though it is not based on any one religion. It keeps me busy for a while.

Drinking is a big problem here on Marakei. People don't drink socially, but in order to get drunk. *Te karewe*, the fermented toddy, is easily obtained or made, and sometimes men make alcohol from yeast. If they have money, they buy Fiji Bitter or Victoria Bitter beer at the local stores in Rawannawi village. It's mainly men who drink on Marakei. It's not seen as socially okay for women to drink. I am told many times, "A man can beat his daughter or wife if he sees or hears of her drinking."

In Tarawa, things are changing. Sometimes I see Kiribati women who've been drinking at the Otintaai Hotel when I'm there, but it's still rare in the late 1990's. I myself never drink out here on Marakei, since I never drink that much, even in the States, and it would sort of screw up the way villagers view me as a foreign woman in their culture. I don't even drink in Tarawa. I'm not up for the social repercussions that drinking would involve for me while living in Kiribati. Oftentimes drinking just happens because of boredom and lack of things to do. Men sit around on *buias* and drink, or they go to the bush and drink away the day. Sometimes you see or hear awful stories of what happens when people drink.

One of the village nurses, Nei Merita, wife of TeNabaruru,

is so used to being beaten up by him when he is drunk that she knows she'll have to hide for at least three days after each incident so her face can heal. The last heinous incident I hear is Ten Tani, her neighbor, tried to find her after his mother and my friend, Nei Moaniti, was worried Nei Merita hadn't come home and her children were wandering around looking for food.

Ten Tani went to the bush looking for Nei Merita. He came back with her wrapped in one of his old lava lavas, having found her not far from one of TeNabaruru's *bwabai* pits. TeNabaruru had raped her and beaten her body so badly she couldn't walk. Tani had to carry her to the road and then come back to get a motorbike to bring her home.

TeNabaruru showed back up a few days later, not having remembered any of it. He'd been so drunk on yeast that he couldn't remember how his wife's face got like that and he accused her of sleeping with other men. Mareko finally has to let her go as a village nurse because she misses so much work due to these domestic disputes. Lots of villagers, and the catechist who fills in on Marakei until a priest comes every few months, try to speak to TeNabaruru to help him stop drinking, but in the two years I'm here, nothing changes except the color of his wife's face and bruises.

Waoreta, one of the policemen, and my neighbor, has a niece named Nei Tahwai, who used to drink. She acquired a reputation on Marakei for being a slut or a prostitute even though she doesn't drink now. She lives with her uncle's family, but it seems like no one wants to let her start over.

The little kids make up a song about her that they sing when they don't think the adults will hear that goes something like, "Nei Tahwai, the drunk, who sleeps with men in the bush." It makes me realize that it's very hard to carve out a new identity for yourself if you stay on a small coral atoll where everyone knows each other or is related to each other. People see her now and remember how she was when she was younger. And though they admit she seems to have changed for the better, her life is essentially written for her. I ask, "Why is this?" and I am told, "No one would marry her now, and no *ataei n'aine*, no young girls, want to be associated with what she represents in villagers' eyes." Everyone looks at her and says, "*E kaawa neiere*, poor girl."

About three months before my time will finish in Peace Corps, my Kiribati language tutor and friend Itabera loses her brother. TeKaben dies of a stroke after being drunk on a six day binge. He is thirty-two. Apparently he was drunk in the classes he was teaching at the junior secondary school as well. He's the second man I've heard of who has died from a drunken binge in the last few months.

CHAPTER TWENTY-ONE

Tuutana's brother, Atanuea, accidentally kills an elderly man in Tarawa while driving a bus for his cousin's bus company. It rocks Tuutana's family on Marakei. Tuutana doesn't believe me when I mention it to her in a letter. She's convinced I have it wrong, and it was their other brother Beniamina, who drinks a lot, not Atanuea. When she hears from another relative, confirming that it was Atanuea, she writes me a letter about how far away from her family and the land she feels.

He'd been driving on a very narrow part of the island road. On Tarawa, there are only two lanes and people go at breakneck speeds and try to pass each other. At the same time, they are trying to beat oncoming traffic, much like they do in many other countries outside the U.S.

He accidentally hit an elderly man on a motorcycle on the causeway who was trying to pass him, and the man died. Atanuea spent three nights in jail. While he sat in jail, his aunt Ieriama got buckets and buckets of fresh fish and food from her store and brought them to the widow's house. Ieriama was the bus company owner's mother. The family is large and extended but always very tight, and Atanuea and his family lived with Ieriama and her family in Tarawa.

At the widow's home Ieriama sat in a chair in the corner, or cross-legged on the floor. She just sat there. The family and all the relatives of the dead man had what amounted to a wake, and Ieriama was the one quiet guest who sat in the corner, representing the family who had killed the man. No one asked anything of her, or demanded an explanation, or got angry. They accepted that she felt the need to pay penance of a sort to them, or that she felt the need to ask for their forgiveness, to somehow let them know that Atanuea and his family were good people, that this was a mistake on his part, one that they were all ashamed by, but that they wanted to atone for their sins and show that they and he were sorry.

All this was left unsaid. Ieriama's presence there and the food and gifts she brought to the house daily sent the message that she herself could not express.

After three days, the widow of the dead man went to the jail and asked the policemen to release Atanuea. He asked for her forgiveness, and she gave it. She decided to take him on as family. The phrase is *"bo ma ngaia,"* which in Kiribati language means to take on as one's relative, the same as a blood relative. They had a large feast with both families, and Atanuea's wife and children joined with the dead man's wife and children. He became like a son to her, and they learned to move on, to build a life together, bound by sorrow, forgiveness, and love. Their hearts were forever widened by the experience. And mine, for having witnessed it.

I am struck by this story and spend time wondering how the widow found it in her heart to forgive him, and not just forgive him, but take him on as family. I thought that seeing him often might reopen the wound, but for her, it allowed the wound to start to scab up and heal. There is an amazing power in forgiveness, allowing us to be stronger, kinder souls.

The widow gave him acceptance, forgiveness, and the responsibility that he has from now on to her as a son and a member of a family, outside the family he was born into. She gave him a form of love and deep wisdom.

I think to myself that if more people had this kind of wisdom, there could be change on a global scale, as the ability to truly forgive is often the basis for making peace. This amazing power of love and forgiveness to overcome tremendous pain touched me, as well as all who knew of and witnessed the events of this one family on Tarawa atoll. It's unfolding reaffirms my belief that hope, love, and forgiveness can always trump pain if given half a chance.

CHAPTER TWENTY-TWO

THE MAIL IS the only lifeline to the outer world from Marakei, save for the two times I am able to patch through a call on the island's government station CB and a ham radio from Australia, so I can talk to Mom and Dad in the States. Sometimes the mail doesn't come on the plane. Sometimes the plane doesn't come on its weekly schedule, and other times, they forget to load the mailbag onto the plane in Tarawa.

Mail is one highlight in my week. I sometimes get packages, and other times letters from friends and family. There are times when all the mail gets bunched up and I get a month's worth of letters in one week; then I may go another few weeks or a month with no mail at all. When there is a logjam somewhere, and no international mail comes, there is always inter-island mail between other volunteers, or Peace Corps staff, and me.

Sometimes all I need is just one letter to spur me on, to push me, to encourage me that what I'm doing is fine, or the right thing for now. Sometimes I just need to connect with an old friend or family member with a letter to keep my spirits up. My friend and fellow volunteer, Kayla, and I write back and forth to each other from Makin island to Marakei, about what is keeping us busy, and keeping us up at night as well.

Every now and then a package arrives from overseas for me. More often, mail gets lost and sent to Papua, New Guinea, or the rats chew through the package and leave me only the wrappers of what was sent. Sometimes, parts of packages arrive intact. When I explain this to my friends and family in the States, they get clever. I receive chocolate frosting in sealed containers, a jar of Planters peanuts, and Tootsie Rolls sent in Tupperware. The audiotape of ocean waves sent to me by a well-meaning friend, and meant for relaxation, perplexes people on Marakei, as it does me. Tuutana's family and I good naturedly laugh about why anyone would listen to a tape of waves when they live fifty feet from the ocean.

If the mailbag comes and Nei Maritaake, the postmaster and CB operator, is not available, it goes to the island clerk's office or house, which is where it is the day I slice my foot open.

The mailbag had come earlier, but Nei Maritaake was nowhere to be found, so someone brought the mailbag to the island clerk's home, which is near my own house in the government station. I run to her house to find out about mail, not seeing the piece of sheet metal sticking out near the side of her buia and slice my foot open between the pinky toe and next toe up, blood spurting everywhere, and my foot flopping open. There was no one even at the clerk's house, so I run, hop, and make my way back to my own house, where I sit on the *buia*, watching the blood for a minute.

Luckily, Brigitte, the other Peace Corps volunteer on Marakei, had just biked to the government station from her village of Tekarakan, to check the mail too. "Oh no, I'm going to go get Mareko," she says to me, immediately biking off in the direction of Emeri and Mareko's house.

By the time Emeri comes to get me on the *repe repe*, I have almost passed out, and by the time we get to the clinic and Mareko stitches me up with the same sutures that the agricultural assistant uses to suture the pigs' testicles when they are sterilized, I am out of it. I stay at the clinic for a few hours and then am brought home.

I try to hobble around on my stitched up foot for a week, but it isn't healing right. The sutures are too big, and it looks infected. After sitting on the sidelines during the Kiribati Independence Day festivities, which go on for a full week in July, I am able to *bubuti* someone to get a seat on the plane into Tarawa, so I can get the Peace Corps nurse to look at my foot and possibly give me antibiotics.

The Peace Corps nurse, Nadine, takes one look at my foot, and says, "Those stitches need to come out, and we need to see what's underneath there, to clean it out." I ask for two volunteer friends to hold my leg while Nadine gives me a shot of Demerol for the pain, and then she calmly cuts the stitches out, while I wince and cry out loud. She cleans out the wound and decides not to re-suture it, but rather to let it just heal on its own, as it isn't flopping open anymore.

I get around on crutches after that and I stay in the capital for a few more weeks while my foot heals. Here, I'm not pining for mail, as I am able to talk on the phone to the States and am able to eat overpriced Western style junk food like ice cream and chocolate that is available on the main island of Tarawa.

Letters from me to the States are plentiful too, with their colorful violet squirrel fish or spinner dolphin stamps on them. I have serious amounts of time to write, as life always moves at a slower pace here. I also read eighty books in two years, using kerosene lanterns to read by at night, or candles bought at the big Catholic church in Tarawa. Some people, including Anterea and Eritabeta, have a few solar-powered lights hanging from the coconut tree beams of their ceilings, but this is not so common. The clinic, where Mareko is headquartered, has a solar powered refrigerator that always seems to be out, or the door is left open, almost ensuring the vaccines are usually not kept cold.

Most people have a combination of kerosene lanterns or they burn coconut oil with homemade wicks for a little light at night on their *buias* or in their homes. I also use my headlamp flashlight to read books by, or to light up the space so I can write more letters.

The twinges of isolation and loneliness I felt in the very beginning of my time on this island that's all about being together and family, eke away as I get closer to Tuutana, and then to her family. It helps to hang out with more young, unmarried people, and some families I get to know well. I think to myself, "Would it make a difference if all I did for two years was befriend people?" I'm not sure I can ever know if I'm useful here, so at least I'm making some wonderful friends.

A few months after moving to New Zealand, Tuutana writes to say she's doing well and that she's now part of a Kiribati dance troupe in Auckland. She sends me a copy of the video of her performing traditional Kiribati dances. Dancing was something she'd apparently steadfastly refused to do (while in Kiribati) since grammar school. She asks me in her enclosed letter to share the video with Anterea and Eritabeta and their kids, "so they can see me in my new 'look.'" Anterea watches, and I see Eritabeta crying softly when she sees on the tape that Tuutana looks healthy and is smiling.

Tuutana writes that, "they are still doing my visa." She says she thinks in Kiribati and translates to *I-Matang* (English) when she talks to New Zealanders. I become the de facto link between Tuutana and some of her friends who don't write letters. Her friends Marenuea and Teretia ask me to say hello to her and tell her their news in my letters to New Zealand. Her sister Karetita asks me to post letters that she doesn't want her father, Anterea, to read, asking for help to pay for her school books. Karetita thinks he'd be embarrassed that she'd asked Tuutana for money.

Anterea and Eritabeta send letters but seem to realize that someone else is now responsible for Tuutana's well-being. They tell me they look forward to hearing more from her about how her life there turns out. Tuutana's biological father, Uni, calls to me from the side of the road while I'm biking in Rawannawi village one day, and asks me to, "please send her a message from me." He wants me to write her to, "please stay, to get work or to study, so that things can go well for you there."

Bauro, Tuutana's boyfriend from the year before, comes out to Marakei a few months later. He has not been in touch with her via phone or letter for a long time. He arrives bringing three pairs of women's soccer cleats from overseas, and lots of camera film. He acts proud and like a "big man on campus" until he hears Tuutana has left, whereupon hearing she's in New Zealand, he looks like he's been hit in the stomach. He says, "*akea te kanganga*" (no problem), but he looks crestfallen. His tour of duty on ship isn't supposed to be over, but he plays it cool saying, "I'm done."

Most villagers know you don't come back from German

or Japanese ships before one year to eighteen months, unless something's wrong and you're booted off. At Emeri and Mareko's house, Bauro acts like he's flirting with me. When I ask him, "What's up? Since either you're Tuutana's boyfriend or you're just being stupid," he doesn't seem to understand that my loyalty is to her, not to him.

CHAPTER TWENTY-THREE

THAT OLD CLICHÉ that "wherever you go, there you are," rings true to what I take to the latrine and well project. I'm anxious for it to all work out the way it's planned on paper; I want this project to be useful to the villagers and to be a helpful *I-Matang*, foreigner working there. Of course, change rarely happens the way we want it to, and in this case, it happens at a much slower, gradual pace.

I try to remember this project is theirs, not mine; nevertheless, the villagers ask me lots of questions about it, have a lot of ideas about what they think *I* should do to help them. I feel responsible. This is a lifelong thing of mine, taking responsibility for things that I should not necessarily be responsible for.

While in training, I learned about the different types of latrines that can be built on the outer islands of Kiribati, where there's no such thing as indoor plumbing or large sanitation systems for human waste. We also learned about the issues of making sure that there is/was proper site placement for latrines and wells, so as to not further contaminate the water supply with human or animal waste. In actuality, the only type of latrine being built on Marakei is the water-seal latrine, a hole covered with cement, dug in the ground, that you squat over to defecate, and that you "flush" with water, usually stored in a bucket with a tin cup (for pouring) placed near the hole. Sometimes there is a plastic piece, like a bowl attached to the cement, but this is rarely the case while I'm there.

The reality is that there usually isn't enough room to have the recommended amount of space between latrines and wells, or animal pens and wells, and most drinking water is contaminated with various parasites on Marakei and all the outer islands, as well as on Tarawa, making it necessary to boil the drinking water.

Since I first arrived on Marakei, I have been asked for assistance in obtaining materials to build latrines. Most people say they want one, even if they themselves don't yet wish to defecate in one, preferring the beach or the bush for this purpose. Health education sessions on using the latrines that are already near some people's homes find an audience that welcomes the information, but are slow to put it into practice. Villagers reason that if the *unimwane*, the old wise men, have the habit of going to the beach or the bush to defecate, then it's okay for everyone else too. I can hear where they're coming from.

Ten Bwakineti, head of the Mother Village Welfare Group (MVWG), brings a request to me that he says is on behalf of all the village welfare groups. They need funding to build more latrines and wells in each of the villages. I talk with Mareko; he thinks "maybe we should ask them if they want latrines and wells for each family, or just next to the *maneabas*, since that is where people congregate for *botakis*, for playing bingo, or watching videos." We know, and the village welfare groups and island council know, that trying to get funding for every household to have their own pit latrine is a multi-year project, one that we may not have access to funding for. Bwakineti and Mareko together ask me, "Can you help us get funding for the cement and labor?" They mean, can I help to try to write or apply for a funding grant from somewhere.

Practically speaking, the villagers can volunteer the labor for building latrines in public places, such as the *maneabas*, the island council office, and the schools. But funding does need to be found for the cement that will be used to make the latrine molds, and the shipping costs to get these bags of cement from Tarawa Supplies out to Marakei.

Bwakineti says, "First try to get funding for latrines and wells near the public meeting places, as this will be a good way to reduce the spread of disease when large groups of people gather. If we are successful in obtaining funding for this project, we can then try to obtain funding for individual latrines on Marakei." I start off optimistically believing this too. It gets voted on by the village welfare groups and approved.

The task of trying to find funding is an interesting one since I, the *I-Matang*, am seen as the bridge to helping write a grant proposal for sources of funds. They know they have their own ministries they can approach, not to mention the island project officer, island development officer, and island water and sanitation worker, who will all be involved at some point, but none of them have much experience with writing grants and would like to learn how anyway, if I could involve them in the process. Given that many of these people and groups are my counterparts, I am asked to help coordinate this project, an assignment given to me by both Mareko and the Mother VWG. The task also partially falls to me because it fits under the description of Peace Corps Rural Health Extension Education Volunteer, my role on Marakei; it's considered part of health promotion and vector control.

There is a valid concern raised in the *maneaba* councils about who will be responsible for maintaining latrines in public places. Discussions take place within the individual wards and villages about different plans to take care of the latrines. Most villages agree that they will buy a padlock and chain in Tarawa, only open the latrines when there are large functions at the longhouses, and that the *maneaba* caretaker can make sure the latrine is not ruined and is taken care of properly. Structures will be built to house the latrines, made up of the same local materials that all homes and buildings are made of: coconut mid-ribs, locally made rope, and pandanus thatch roofs.

Anote, the convicted rapist, gets wind of this project, and he's mad. He comes to Marakei one weekend, upset with a lot of people, including me. Though approval was gained by consensus in the village *maneaba* meetings, Anote is upset he hasn't been consulted or asked for money. He says, "I don't want the government to help in something I can finance myself." According to one of the other Peace Corps volunteers, who has heard it on rumor, "he wants to kick you off the island," but then I have heard rumors before that he wants all Peace Corps volunteers to leave Kiribati.

Anote says he can fund the latrines himself. He comes to my house one night, before I've locked up, barges in with one of his supporters, and lunges towards me. But then he says, "I want to talk with you tomorrow in the *maneaba*." He seems drunk that night, and his friend Keakea takes him away.

I meet with him the next day in the island council

maneaba, where he is holding court. He is polite to me, though he reiterates his points from the night before, which have to do with him not thinking I have a role on Marakei and funding the latrines himself.

When I talk about this with the village welfare groups the next day and later that week, they tell me, "Ignore Anote, and go ahead with what we talked about previously." Nevertheless, they still take the money Anote bribes them with here and there.

Some of the village *maneabas* need wells built nearby if they are building a latrine. I write a grant proposal to the Ministry of Health and Family Planning. I detail costs, including the volunteer contribution of labor and materials to build "housing" for the latrines, and the plan for taking care of the latrines near the longhouses, the schools, and the island council office. The island clerk, which is equivalent to the mayor of Marakei, the head of the Mother VWG, and Mareko all sign off on the grant proposal and it gets shipped off. The total cost of the project comes to $1486.00.

After several months, a letter finally comes back, saying that the ministry approves of the project, but that the amount asked for is considered too small; therefore, they will not be funding it. They state in their letter that they only fund projects for more than $5000. Village welfare group leaders, Mareko and I are all disappointed, but decide to retool the grant proposal to fit into the format needed to apply for a small Peace Corps funding source that assists the villages and islands that have Peace Corps Volunteers in their area to obtain smaller sums of money for small project assistance projects. We fill out countless forms, I file them, and we eventually receive word that Peace Corps has approved funding for the project and will send sixty-six bags of cement on the next ship to Marakei.

Despite the best efforts to convene a meeting of the various parties involved in this project, all our meetings never stay on track and things move slowly. Human connections are always more important than accomplishments here, and this is a good reminder for me in my life and time here. Things need to happen on Kiribati-time since it was a project they had initiated because they wanted help with it.

Assistance is needed from the water and sanitation technician, Te Enri, who is drunk most of the time. In addition, there is a faulty latrine mold, according to him, that has been shipped out to Marakei. Half of the latrines he makes with the cement crack when he takes them off the mold and then he has to start all over.

I am antsy for some progress to be made and know I should be learning lessons about cultural pace, and letting things unfold naturally, which eventually happens by default anyway.

My Peace Corps service is coming to an end in December, a few months away. There is a local man named Ten Nemeia who can also make the molds for the wells. Apparently, he had stolen the ring mold from the island council several years earlier. They have been unable—or not tried (I am not sure)—to get it back from him. I spend a few weeks gently needling Ten Nemeia first, to make the molds for each village. I go to his house, I ask him nicely, I *bubuti* him, I plead.

When I arrive at Ten Nemeia's stone and cement Western-style house, I am met by one of his sons. The other sons appear to be doing nothing at all; they are sitting cross-legged or lying on the cement floor. Flies are being swatted from plastic bowls of fried fish by two of the old man's daughters-in-law. The *unimwane*, the old man, Ten Nemeia, looks at me and I feel sweat beading on my upper lip.

"Please could you be so kind as to make the ring molds for the seven village wells? I say in my foreigner's version of Kiribati language.

I mention nothing about the fact that he stole the ring mold from the government council. I stare out the open window, waiting for his response, and see the extended clan's laundry drying on the line outside. Sitting there, I catch a glimpse of a few other daughters-in-law doing more wash by hand in large aluminum basins. Even as I say this, I know my coming here to speak to him will get around to everyone, as all news travels quickly on the "coconut wireless."

"When do you want them done?" he asks. When I say, "As soon as possible please," he says, "Kiribati time," and I groan inwardly; that means it won't happen anytime soon.

"*I keve*, I'm joking," he says, both to me and his sons, with an impish grin. "I will do them as soon as possible."

"*Ko rabwa*, thank you, thank you very much," I say, and manage to stand up, gathering my skirt up from around me on the floor.

A month before my two years of service is up, villages have wells and latrines and the project seems to be wrapping up. There are no final meetings or any acknowledgment of what we've accomplished.

CHAPTER TWENTY-FOUR

I EVENTUALLY GIFT MY pig, WilburTwo to Teria and TeRui for their son's first birthday *botaki*, a month before leaving Marakei, as a way of thanking them for helping me with so many things. They are the last policeman and wife to reside in the house right next door to mine.

There are going away *botakis* for me. There is one with the Mother *Kamwengaraoi*, where they sing one of the two Marakei island anthems, and I walk around the longhouse saying goodbye to all of my friends. I have tears streaming down my face as I wind up back where Mareko and Emeri are sitting. They have been such a big part of my life.

The last day on Marakei, I wake early and take down the mosquito net I'd strung on the big coconut beams holding my house together. Standing on the plank I'd laid my Therm-a-Rest on for two years; I look at what has been my home.

Karetita comes with breakfast for me from Eritabeta, her mother, who knew I would have no food left in my house on this last day. Boiled breadfruit and dried salt fish.

My neighbor, Nei Teria, comes to help me pack the last of my things and give me a beautiful *tibuta* blouse she's smocked for me as a going-away gift. Never mind that her baby is crying to nurse.

We take the handcart, and all that I will keep from a little more than two years, and we take turns pushing my cargo to the small house on the airstrip, which serves as the airport and waiting area for planes. Planes sometimes come hours or days late, are often grounded for maintenance, and are rarely reliable.

Beatirike comes to say goodbye with her boys, the youngest I've watched learn to walk and talk and call my name. This boy, Nanataake, has become a regular "passenger" on the bar of my bicycle. As he began to look at me as another adult family member, he could and would travel around the island and villages with me, perched on his metal bar "seat."

Nei Tekua, a friend, who is also close to my age, comes with Karetita. Karetita had returned home after bringing me breakfast, to help with the feeding of pigs, cleaning and gutting that morning's fresh fish, and boiling the morning's fresh toddy. Now she is back with Tekua.

Slowly, this band of women, Nei Teria, Nei Tekua, Nei Beatirike, Karetita, and I, begin to make our way with the handcart down the main village road. From out of the houses and longhouses come people wanting to say goodbye, to wish me good luck, safe travels…to tell me, "We'll miss you," or to ask me to, "come back and visit." Some I know well; some I think just want me to remember them, and I think I will try to remember everyone and everything about this.

By the time I've made it to the middle ward/section of the village, I am sobbing. Erika, one of the village nurses

I've worked with, gives me a big bear hug and I get a sinking feeling, realizing I am leaving what has become home.

We stop at Karetita's house and Eritabeta, her mother, and my adopted one, comes out to walk with us to the airport. She has baby Bwatiata on one hip and two flower garlands for me in her hand. "One for your neck and one for your head," she tells me. Others who are family will meet us at the airport.

We wait for what seems an eternity. Finally, a couple of hours after it is supposed to arrive, the plane comes and there is a mad rush to get all my cargo on board, and to say final goodbyes to everyone. To hug and kiss the babies I've seen born, to tell those I love goodbye. All with the wrenching feeling that I might never see these people again.

I am just bawling when saying my last goodbyes to Emeri and Mareko. I walk out onto the airstrip, holding baby Bwatiata in my arms and a huge heavy bag on my shoulder. I walk towards the plane with this child I'd helped Eritabeta take care of since the day she was born on her mother's mat the year before. I am like an honorary aunt. Eritabeta, the earth mother center of my world and feeling of home, tells me, "We love you." She says, "You'll always be our child." At the three small steps up to the interior of the prop plane, I hand baby Bwatiata back to Eritabeta, and she and I fall into each other, holding each other and crying uncontrollably. Karetita stands in the background watching her mother and me.

The door to the plane shuts, the villagers move back to the house that is the airport, and the plane takes off down the short airstrip.

It takes seconds to clear the tops of the coconut trees, and I begin to see the outline of this beautiful pear-shaped island in the Pacific with its green ring of trees, sky blue lagoon in the middle, surrounded by cobalt blue ocean on the outside. I can see people from the villages and those I love getting smaller and smaller in the distance. Eritabeta has told me just as I was getting on the plane, "We will see you when you return someday." As the rubber-band engine propels me away from my home on Marakei, I wonder when that will be.

CHAPTER TWENTY-FIVE

After my Peace Corps service ends, I head to New Zealand to travel around on a camping and hiking-type trip. I go to the South Island to travel after seeing Tuutana and her family for the first two days. I will come back three weeks later to stay with them again for a visit.

Back with Tuutana and her grandparents, Karorina and Martin, we go to the ocean in Auckland and hang out. Tuutana seems a little less shell-shocked but has gained some weight. She is not playing soccer and is staying home, helping Karorina, her grandmother (who is essentially her mother here), take care of the children and the house. This is often what happens in Kiribati as well, once the girls get married. The diet on the islands is such that if there is no exercise or awareness of salt and sugar and fat, there is a high incidence of obesity, hypertension, and diabetes. In that sense, it's not different than the often commonly consumed standard American diet of less than healthy food choices.

The diseases of obesity and hypertension and diabetes are mostly linked to an increase in consumption of white rice and refined sugars and flour, none of which are indigenous to Kiribati. This same unhealthy diet is being consumed by Tuutana's family in Auckland. The villagers on Marakei often would say "there was no food" when Marakei was running low on flour, sugar, rice. As if that was all there was. They had always lived off the land until the British came and introduced these things to the I-Kiribati people. Tuutana's family in Auckland seems to think the same way, only they *really* can't live off the land there. My lived experience in the States was also full of many prepackaged and not fresh ingredients, supplemented by fresh foods and fish.

We all go together to a Pacific Islands dance festival. Dancers from all the islands of Micronesia, Polynesia, and Meganesia dance. I help get Tuutana dressed in her costume. She is very good at dancing traditional Kiribati dances now.

When it's time for me to leave and say goodbye, Tuutana is crying. Everyone's crying. It's a big cry fest. We tell each other we'll write and I say I'll phone Tuutana from the States.

I return to the States after twenty-seven months. I go back to my parents' home in Minnesota, in January 2000, and reconnect with family and friends. There's lots of snow, and it's cold beyond belief. I get a job in public health research, and it is so boring it brings tears to my eyes.

Readjustment stinks. It is worse than the adjustment to Kiribati in the first place. I am overwhelmed by Target and the grocery store. At a baby shower for my friend Leora, I make the list of gifts and who gave them, so she can have the information for writing thank you notes later. I am bewildered by the large number of gifts she receives and things a woman supposedly needs to have a baby in the States, such as bouncy seats, strollers (multiple kinds), toys, clothes, carriers, and privacy breastfeeding shields.

In Kiribati, the women made a baby mat; nothing else was done to prepare for the baby. Perhaps they got someone to buy them *bitakis* (changing cloths made of all-purpose soft cotton to use as diapers, towels, burp cloths). As for breastfeeding privacy screens, no one thought anything on Marakei of a woman just hiking up her shirt anywhere and breastfeeding.

I speak with Tuutana on the phone from Minnesota. She hints that this same sense of being overwhelmed is somewhat true for her in New Zealand as well. She says, "I'm constantly seeing new things that are different from those on Marakei."

I am realizing that being in a culture with a slower pace, where life is a little more predictable, was a gift. But the greatest gift included being with people whom I learned to love and who loved me as well. Though that could happen with family at home, it felt very profound on Marakei. There Eritabeta told people who asked why I came to their house so much, "Amy is our *natira (child)*." When these same people said, "*Eng*, yes?" she said, "*Eng*, yes, because she's Tuutana's sister." I realize that Marakei widened my heart.

I move to California. Tuutana wants to know why I would move where I don't have family. I want to live in a warmer climate, in a city with a larger Jewish population, and I get a library job in Los Angeles. After Marakei, I know that I will find a good community of friends and support by being willing to try and find people with whom I can connect wherever I am.

CHAPTER TWENTY-SIX

M Y FRIEND AND fellow Peace Corps health education volunteer, Kayla, and I talk about going back to visit friends on our respective islands in Kiribati. We start talking about planning for summer 2003. I miss family and friends on Marakei. I was concerned they wouldn't write to me when I left, and some haven't. But now it's me who doesn't write often, and worries that my Kiribati language, which was never as great written as it was spoken, is lacking. I feel disconnected from their lives while I carve out my life here in Los Angeles. With Tuutana, I can call her in New Zealand and catch up on news of her life. She sometimes finds out news from Marakei from Kiribati seamen whose ships stop in Auckland.

Tuutana says on the phone that she is both, "*kukurei* and *nanokawaki* (both happy and sad)" because she has family there and will be able to get work there when her permanent visa is granted, and yet she misses, "the land, her family, the *bwabwai*, the breadfruit, the fish, and the Kiribati customs of Marakei." Mostly, she says she misses "*te aba*," the land.

She tells me she hangs out with mostly Kiribati friends in Auckland, and she is still waiting for permanent visa status. When she gets her permanent visa, she'll go back to visit Marakei. She says, "To visit, Amy, *tiaki bukin te tiku*, to visit, not to stay." She would like to work at the metalworks factory where most of her family works in Auckland.

I start a second master's degree program, an MFA in creative writing at Antioch Los Angeles. I do this while I am working as a children's librarian at the Jewish Community Library. At the same time, I'm in a relationship with a guy named Anthony that is starting to have issues and tension. We get engaged at the point where, in hindsight, we should have broken up. After being engaged for eight months, he gets scared and calls off the wedding, close to the actual date.

Anthony and I had planned to go to Fiji, New Zealand, and Kiribati on our honeymoon, and I decide to take the trip still, with my friend, Kayla.

My connection to Kiribati after having lived there for two years is still strong and I would like to visit my adoptive family there. and we had booked the flights for a five-week honeymoon trip. When the wedding gets called off, I ask Anthony to sign his overseas airline ticket over to Kayla, which he does. I would still be taking the trip, albeit two weeks shorter, and more rustic, than originally planned. I figure I might as well take a great trip.

He and I meet at the Delta International ticket counter at LAX one night after work, a week after his, "I want to marry you, but I don't think we should" line. He signs over his ticket to Kayla, and I change the Fiji portion to a shorter trip, to head back to the States through New Zealand, so I can see Tuutana.

I ask him to please fax a letter to the Air Nauru representatives at LAX, so I can get the Fiji to Kiribati tickets transferred over as well. The young woman at the Air Afrique counter, which doubles as the Air Nauru booking office is perplexed. "Who spends thousands of dollars on a wedding, and a couple thousand just on airline tickets alone to get to this tiny little island country no one has ever heard of, just to change their mind a few weeks beforehand?" she asks me, and I have no good answer. I am also still hurt. But I am excited to take the trip, and figure it will be good for me to get away for a while.

Kayla is happy too. All she has to pay for is the change fee and the $500 portion from Fiji to New Zealand. At least Kayla and I get something out of it. Kayla was one of my best friends in the Peace Corps. She's now a 71-year-old retired public health nurse; she did more in her two years on the island of Makin while in her later sixties, than many younger volunteers all put together.

Here in the States, Kayla and I have visited each other in the Southern part of New York state, and Southern California a few times in the past few years. Though we may go for a few months in between speaking on the telephone, we shared such an intense part of our lives for those two years that we always pick right back up and seem to know exactly how the other may have coped with what new events are going on in our respective lives.

When Kayla and I step off the plane at Bonriki International Airport on Tarawa, we are struck by the intense heat we'd left behind four years before and forgotten. Back on the equator again, I immediately peel off layers of clothes, and mop the sweat off my face. In the "customs" line, which doubles as the baggage and inspection line as well, I am surprised to see young girls, *ataei n'aine*, wearing jeans and shorts, which had been *tabuaki* (taboo) five years earlier amongst most single, unmarried girls and women.

"*Nei* Amy, *Nei* Amy, *Nei* Amy Ooooo!" I hear through the slats that separate the inspection line area we are in from the outside "public" area. I look over and see *Nei* Tetiria and *Nei* Karetita (Anterea and Eritabeta's daughter-in-law and daughter respectively) jumping up and down on the other side to get my attention. I wander over to them and we greet each other, "*Mauri*, Hello!" through the slats. Then I ask if they've heard from Anterea that Anthony isn't coming (that I came alone, save for Kayla, who will be going on to visit the island she'd served as a Peace Corps Volunteer while I visit Marakei). "*Eti, Amy, am reta e a ti bwa roko n te wiki aei.* Yes, Amy, your letter just arrived this week."

We wind up taking a bus to the Otintaai Hotel, the only real "Western" style hotel in Kiribati. I immediately remember and recognize the smells of morning cooking fires and the lagoon at low tide. Some things never change, because after four years, the same front desk person still can't find the key to our room and housekeeping has to let us in. The water at the hotel is working intermittently, and I remember that feeling of standing with soap in your hair under a shower head that has just run out of water from when we would sometimes stay here during Peace Corps all-volunteer conferences.

In other ways though, the whole country seems different. There are the clothes that people wear, Tarawa seems much more crowded than I remember, people are carrying Discmans, and there are some actual restaurants that have cropped up along the one main island road. Later that day, after settling into the room, and taking my first bucket bath since I left the country four years earlier, I mention to Tetiria that I'd seen a couple of drunk girls wandering in Tarawa. This was previously, even four years beforehand, considered grounds for their husbands, fathers, or some male family member to beat them, as it was also *tabuaki* for girls to drink alcohol. It was not good that girls were subjected to abuse for drinking, but I am just noting the cultural shift as a visitor who had lived here years before. Tetiria says to me, "*E roko te katei mai itinaniko,* Amy. It's come, the culture from overseas," she said. And I notice that in the years I've been away, a movie theater has come to Betio, and a small dial-up access internet café (solely on Tarawa, not on outer islands) has also come. There are more stores with some overseas canned foods, and a lot more cars and buses on the one road traversing the capital island of Tarawa.

I spend a couple pleasant days in Tarawa, visiting with Tetiria and family, eating chunks of raw yellowfin tuna drenched in freshly grated and squeezed coconut milk, before I can get a seat on the weekly plane to Marakei. Before I leave, Tetira and I talk. She asks, "Why didn't you get married?" She said Anterea and his wife, Eritabeta, "were looking forward to seeing you again, and meeting your husband." They'd been planning on it for months, ever since Anthony and I had sent that first letter to tell them we would be coming. It was as though their foreign daughter, coming home with the husband who had never met them, would have been honoring them. It would have been. All I can say to Tetiria was what I wrote in my letter to Anterea, "Me too. I was looking forward to it too. But he changed his mind. *E aoraki burona.* He was sick in his heart." And it was true. He was sick at heart and couldn't get married. Tetiria seems satisfied with that, but then just launches into, "Why don't you find a Kiribati husband now?"

On Tarawa, I also see my old friends Emeri and Mareko. It is a fluke that I even see them, because they are only in Tarawa for a few weeks. They are now stationed on the island of Abaiang, but Mareko has a training at the sole hospital for the thirty-three islands that make up the country of Kiribati. As an example of how one can randomly run into people or find out information about people easily in a country of only about 80,000, I had asked around at Nawerewere, the hospital, to see if anyone knew Mareko Kaibwebwe and where he was living now. Sure enough, someone offers to take me to the back bush road out towards his land near the airport. I meet Mareko's new son, who is about three years old, and I see how the children who had hung out in my house every day for two years are now older. Reconnecting with Mareko and Emeri brings back a flood of warm feelings for a family, with whom there had been so many emotions and interactions back at the time.

After a few days in Tarawa, I take the sole plane in the country to Marakei island. It is the same plane I'd flown in years ago, "The Y12," it was called. Back then it was rubber-banded together, so I wonder how much more so now? Picture old prop planes, where they balance the eighteen passengers and their luggage to make sure the plane can fly, where every single part has been repaired or replaced at some point in its twenty-five to thirty-year life span. That's flying in Kiribati.

Four hours past its scheduled arrival time, the Tarawa-Marakei plane arrives. I get on with the same agricultural assistant from years ago, who is still the island's agricultural assistant, and a bunch of other villagers whom I know and who remember me. It is a bit like going back to a small hometown where everyone knows who you are. "Amy, *ko uringai*? Amy, do you remember me?" the older ones ask, and flash their toothless grins at me. I mostly do remember them.

When the plane has Marakei in sight, I find myself tearing up and staring hard out the window, trying to gauge if what I have remembered will be the same. Four years ago, when my Peace Corps service came to an end, when Eritabeta hugged me and said, "We'll see you when you come back," I had wondered if I would ever make the journey back. Now, I can see the small house that is the airport, people standing around it, and the lagoon, sparkling blue, in the middle of the island.

Eritabeta meets me at the airport this time, too. We hug, cry, and walk back through the village to her and Anterea's home. It feels like going home. Walking through Rawannawi village, I hear calls of "*Ko oki,* Amy? You came back, Amy?" "*I oki, I oki.* I came back. I came back," I reply. And then they laugh and joke about how I haven't forgotten my Kiribati language or the island of Marakei. The language keeps coming back to me the more I speak it with friends.

Sitting on the *buia,* the open air porch, at Eritabeta's house, eating more raw fish and freshly caught land crabs and just harvested *bwabwai,* swamp taro, I talk to Anterea and Eritabeta. They have the same manner about them as I remembered from before, happy for your happiness, and gently raised eyebrows when they hear something disappointing. They remind me that so much of what happens in our lives is not really in our control or even necessarily fair and I find their reminding me of this is comforting. The tides, money, food, health, are all controlled by forces such as nature, God, and the spirits in Kiribati and the conversation reminds me of that.

The nice thing about going back is that they don't make as big of a deal about me as if I'd been new to the island. When I'd first arrived in Marakei in 1997, each group affiliated with the island council or village welfare had volleyed to host a *botaki* for me. I was pulled in different directions by different groups who wanted time with the new Peace

Corps health volunteer. Right away this time, I get to just hang out and go to the *maneaba*, and to play bingo with the women in the family and the village ward that first evening. Before bed every night, we all *tebo-tebo*, bucket bathe, in the latrine, get into clothes that double as pajamas, and then sit by the *moon-tiger* (mosquito coils) to play dominoes, while Radio Kiribati relates news of the various islands. Every so often, Nei Uereti, the old woman in the family, or Eritabeta, will click their teeth and say, "*Ana koraki Ten Betero*," or "*e kaawa*," meaning, "that person whose name was announced is the family of Ten Betero, or it's so sad," if someone's name is announced as having just died.

Radio Kiribati and CB radios transmit most of the news between islands. Because people do move a lot, or are from Marakei island, but live, for example, on Tarawa or Abaiang for work or marriage, then announcing things on the radio is how they find out the news. This means that people who move also announce things on the radio. It's how people know how their family is doing, who has recently died, what cargo ships are going to what islands and which month or day, or if the plane will be coming. I fall asleep every night of my "going back visit" on Marakei to sounds of the radio and the pigs squealing, snug in my mosquito net, and feeling loved and surrounded by family and friends.

I notice on Marakei, that though many of the latrines we built when I was a Peace Corps volunteer are no longer functioning, most people now have a latrine of their own, or near their home. And my unscientific observation makes me think they're being used more now than four years before.

Anteria isn't able to make it to the airport to see me off when I leave Marakei, as he is teaching in school that morning. He tells me at the house early that morning, "I hope it was good for you to come home. We're glad to have had you." And when Eritabeta and all the kids walk me to the airstrip to leave, I tell her, "*Ko rabwa ibukin te motirrawa ikai iriarikimi E toki teutana, te nanokawaki.* Thank you for the time here with you. It stopped a little, the sadness, (the missing you, the sadness of recent life changes, etc.) while I was here." I thank her again for welcoming me home. It was healing.

Eritabeta stands stoically by the cinder block airport house, occasionally waving and watching the plane start to rev its engine. I wave back. She's surrounded by her daughter, Karetita, her other children, and more kids from the village. Young children play in the dust and on old bicycles in the dirt, waiting to see the plane take off. Women sit on their haunches under the shade of a pandanus tree, picking nits from each other's hair. The plane lurches forward, and begins to move down the dirt airstrip, before doubling back again past the house to gather speed. I see Eritabeta waving at the plane, and I wave back, though by now we've taken off over the vast Pacific Ocean. As I watch the frame of her body fade in the distance through the small plasticized plane window, I think to myself, "I don't know if I'll ever make it back here, but in some ways, a part of me never left."

Kayla and I have a stopover in Auckland, where we stay in a hotel, but I see Tuutana, and she brings me a basket of goodies when she greets me at the airport. By then, she is working as a nanny for a family in the city. I bring her a letter from Anterea, which she chooses to share with me; in it, he reminds Tuutana that she will always be their child, that she needs to keep moving forward with her life, and that he and Eritabeta love her very much, and to stay in touch with me because we are sisters now too.

CHAPTER TWENTY-SEVEN

I CAUGHT THE BOUQUET at my friend Lena's wedding last weekend. Lena is the friend I lit Hanukkah candles with while we were in the Peace Corps in Kiribati. Though her wedding takes place in the Columbia River Gorge area of Oregon, it is decidedly Kiribati in style. She has Kiribati dancers, a group of maybe twenty Kiribati natives scattered and living across the Pacific Northwest, from Concord, California to Vancouver, British Columbia. She has Kiribati twist music that the DJ plays. Former volunteers from our original group include me, Marina, and Andrea. A few others can't make it but send greetings in Kiribati to Lena and Scott: "*tekeraoi n taai nako*, good luck forever," and the traditional wishes and greetings, "*Te mauri, te raoi, ao te tabomoa*, Health, good things, and prosperity to you."

Though I know there is a smattering of I-Kiribati people living in the States, I've never met any here before. In Oregon, I find out there's a small population. In all of the United States, Hawaii has the highest concentration of I-Kiribati nationals, because of its proximity to the Central

Pacific island country. Hawaii itself is still a day's worth of travel from Kiribati by plane. Lena's wedding puts me in touch with some of the Kiribati people in the States and reminds me how my own life was so much calmer and slower while living on Marakei than it is in California now.

After graduating with my MFA in December 2004, I continue working at the library and working on some writing projects. I am trying to find a way to weave all my experiences together and use the skills for something good.

I still talk with Tuutana on the phone, or we write back and forth. She had wanted to go back to Kiribati, but ended up in Fiji. She stays with her Uncle Tion and his wife Ekera, who are Kiribati, but live part of the time in Fiji, and part of the time in Betio, a part of Tarawa, in Kiribati.

In Fiji, she meets a guy named Juni, who is from Rabi, a Fijian island, that is made up of Kiribati islanders who were originally from Banaba Island. When the last of the phosphate was mined out of Banaba, the people of Banaba were relocated to Rabi. There, even though they are in Fiji, they speak Kiribati. To be more precise, only one of Juni's parents was Kiribati, and the other is Fijian, so Tuutana refers to him as half-Kiribati. Tuutana and he are married.

We email back and forth, Tuutana and I, and I stay in touch with my fellow Peace Corps Kiribati friends.

Two years in Kiribati, on Marakei, helped give me wonderful loving individuals who are a part of my life and heart, and it helped me calm my mind. But now I am on the path to finding healthy ways to do all of that without having to make such a radical shift as moving halfway across the world and living in a stick hut.

Years after I leave Marakei, I find a good combination of job and friends and community. Years after that, because life is a process of trying to improve one's character and who they are, I find a more robust support system and a deeper connection to God. I find myself happy and peaceful on a regular basis; life is good, despite stresses that come my way. This is even better than what I found on Marakei. I am ever grateful for that experience, as it allowed me to have a glimpse of what peace and stability could look like in my life, and gave me wonderful, lifelong friends.

As for Tuutana, she is happily married and living on Suva, in Fiji. Her sister Karetita, Anterea and Eritabeta's oldest child together, is living in Australia and working as a nurse. She is married with children of her own. Occasionally, we are in touch via facebook messenger. In the earlier years, shortly after I had left Marakei, Karetita and I would Skype together from time to time, and Tuutana and I would email each other.

My Kiribati language is beginning to fade, since I have little use for it in my everyday life in Southern California. My friends from Marakei and I are less in touch than we used to be. Even though I no longer dream in Kiribati and there isn't the opportunity to speak the language and communicate with my friends and family there, I carry the experiences, memories, and people from Marakei and the Republic of Kiribati with me wherever I go. They help to warm my heart.

PHOTO ALBUM

1 Amy standing by the Peace Corps sign in Tarawa

2 Amy dancing traditional Kiribati dance in a maneaba (longhouse)

3 Luggage to Marakei

4 Marakei view from the plane

5 Spirit Statue

6 Amy's house, exterior

MY PEACE CORPS ODYSSEY | 153

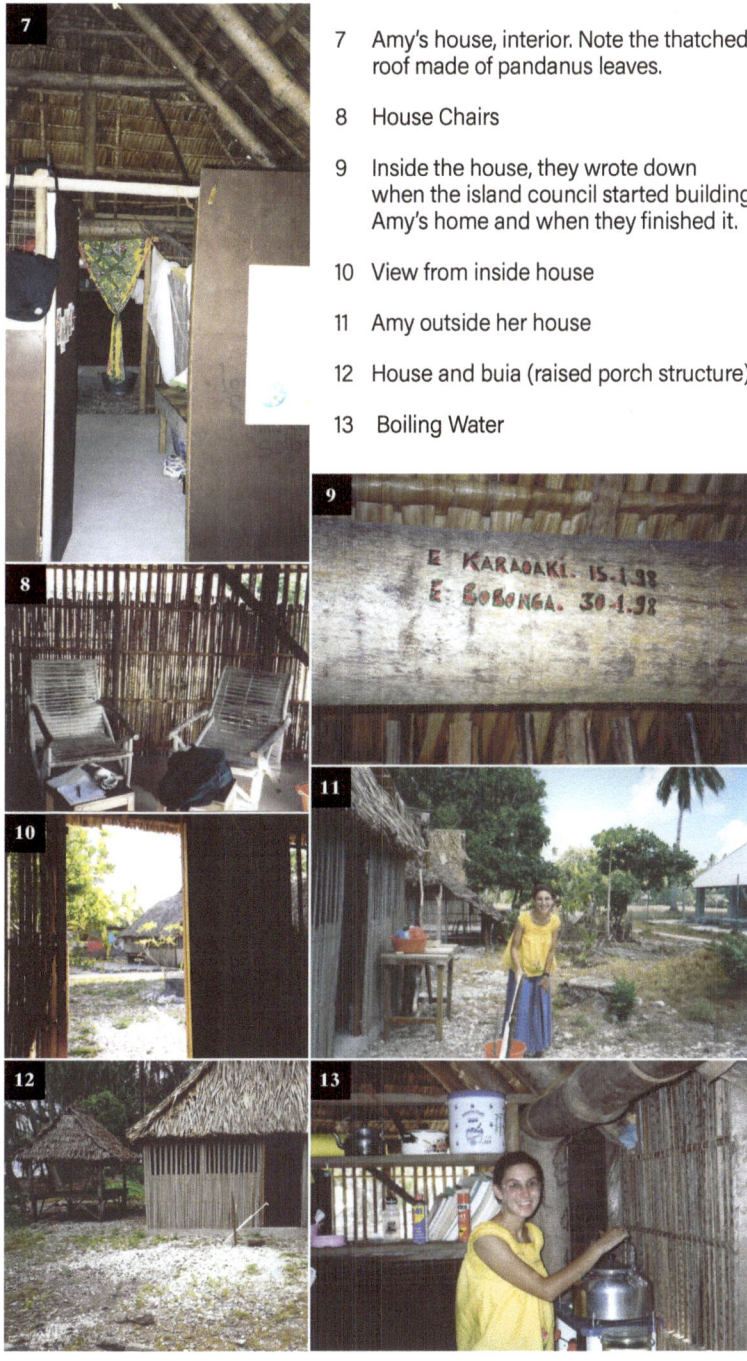

7   Amy's house, interior. Note the thatched roof made of pandanus leaves.

8   House Chairs

9   Inside the house, they wrote down when the island council started building Amy's home and when they finished it.

10 View from inside house

11 Amy outside her house

12 House and buia (raised porch structure)

13 Boiling Water

14 Amy in the hammock

15 Pit latrine

16 Mosquito net

17 Laundry day

18 Ocean view from outside house

19 Amy on the motorbike

20 Amy's garden

21 Marakei road

22 Amy by Antai village

23 Amy by the bwabwai (giant swamp taro)

24 Woman making rope made from the webbing inside of the coconut

25 Bwabwai (view from above)

26 Papaya from a neighbor's tree

27 Amy's pet pig, Wilbur

28 Octopus drying to be salted and eaten later

29 Octopus meal

30 Pumping water

31 Amy on her buia

32 Sparkly birthday dress they made Amy for her 28th birthday botaki

33 Patient ward at Marakei island's main health clinic

34 Marakei seashore